Bible
Folding Stories

Old Testament Stories and Paperfolding Together As One

Christine Petrell Kallevig

photographs by Eric Skarl

International

P. O. Box 470505, Broadview Heights, Ohio 44147

13347935

By the same author:

Folding Stories: Storytelling and Origami Together As One

Holiday Folding Stories: Storytelling and Origami Together For
    Holiday Fun

All About Pockets: Storytime Activities For Early Childhood

Storytime Ink International
P. O. Box 470505, Broadview Heights, Ohio 44147

ISBN 0-9628769-4-1

Illustrations by Christine Petrell Kallevig
Photographs by Eric Skarl.

First Edition
10 9 8 7 6 5 4 3 2 1
Printed in the United States of America

Library of Congress Catalog Card Number: 93-085089

ACKNOWLEDGMENTS
Biblical text was based on Thomas Nelson & Sons 1952 Revised Standard Version of
The Holy Bible.

Procedure for folding the dove was learned from Andrea Urton in *50 Nifty Origami
Crafts,* (Lowell House Juvenile, Los Angeles, 1992), p. 66.

Procedures for folding the traditional house, cup, and robe were learned from Isao
Honda in *The World Of Origami*, (Japan Publication Trading Co., 1965).

Procedure for folding the fish was learned from Lillian Oppenheimer and Shari
Lewis in *Folding Paper Puppets,* (Stein and Day Publishers, New York, 1962), p. 25.

Procedure for folding the basket was learned from Paul Jackson in *The Complete
Origami Course,* (Gallery Books, New York, 1989), p. 27.

Procedure for folding the baby was learned from Toshie Takahama in *Quick & Easy
Origami*, (Kodansha International, 1988), p. 42.

The author expresses appreciation to...

Rev. Thomas P. O'Brien, Associate Pastor of John Knox Presbyterian Church, North Olmsted, Ohio; Rev. Patrick J. O'Connor, Associate Pastor of St. Basil Catholic Church, Brecksville, Ohio; and Rabbi Daniel A. Roberts of Temple Emanu El, University Heights, Ohio; for their scholarly and insightful evaluations of the stories.

David Kallevig, for his enthusiastic support.

Eric Skarl, for his creative and sensitive photography skills.

This book is dedicated to the memory of Lillian Oppenheimer, the grand lady of American origami. May her generous spirit eternally feed our souls.

About the cover: The origami model featured on the front cover is a large version of Joseph's robe. It was folded out of a 24 inch square of freezer wrap that was first decorated with wide-tipped markers. In order to get a square that large, two rectangles of freezer wrap, each 24 inches by 12 inches, were taped together, forming a middle seam. This procedure worked with this model because it has several layers when finished, effectively concealing the seam. See page 36 for complete folding directions.

TABLE OF CONTENTS

Old Testament stories and paperfolding...
An exciting combination!

A skill common to top educators is the ability to use innovative techniques and materials to invigorate their lessons, creating an exciting and lively learning environment. Biblical text, like many other subjects, can not be altered, but successful religious educators know that the manner in which it is presented can certainly be as dynamic and entertaining as today's sophisticated audiences expect and demand.

One way to spark fresh interest in old stories is to present them in a new way. Using progressive paperfolding, or origami *(the ancient Japanese folk art of folding paper into objects)*, to illustrate stories is an innovation that I've been developing during the last several years. In my previous books, I referred to this technique as *Storigami.*

Storytelling + Origami = Storigami.

In other words, while you tell a story, you also fold paper into different shapes that depict or complement the action, setting, or characters. When the story is over, a simple, three dimensional paper object is also complete. Listeners' minds automatically pair the story events with the folds, so while they enjoy the stories, they also learn how to construct their own paper creations.

The Biblical text in this, my third, collection of folding stories helps to teach simple paperfolding techniques, but the paperfolding techniques also reinforce memory for the Biblical text. The text and the paperfolding are learned simultaneously and painlessly.

Bible Storigami provides an interesting and novel activity for religious classes, celebrations, camps, or events. Emphasis is placed on wholesome fun and creative achievement for both children and adults. Initially, the enjoyment of Storigami comes as listeners visualize and respond to the scenes presented by the storyteller. The pleasure returns as listeners allow their fingers to recapture the images by folding paper of their own.

Learning how to fold a new paper model is not a momentary thrill, but a gift that can be shared with others again and again. When the steps are learned and remembered along with Biblical text, as in the Bible folding stories that follow, then the Biblical text can easily be shared with others, too.

What are the educational benefits of Storigami?

1. *Improved listening skills:* Paperfolding adds interest and grabs attention. Listeners are curious and motivated to pay close attention to the stories and the Biblical text.

2. *Opportunities to practice right cerebral hemisphere visualization skills:* Listeners imagine the scenes described in the stories and understand the symbolic representations of the progressive origami folds. Researchers believe that this ability is related to skills located in the right brain, an area sometimes overlooked in conventional learning tasks.

3. *Opportunities to practice left cerebral hemisphere language comprehension skills:* Listeners understand the words used in the plot, characters, dialog, and setting. Language comprehension is a skill that is located primarily in the left brain.

4. ***Emphasis is placed on multi-sensory, integrated whole brain learning techniques:*** Visual, tactile, and auditory senses are all combined to provide the right and left cerebral hemispheres with input, resulting in an atmosphere of whole-brain learning. Learning is most effective when several areas of the brain are activated simultaneously.

5. ***Memory enhancement:*** Short term memory is improved through paired associations (story events with folding steps) and multi-sensory presentations.

6. ***Improved fine motor skills:*** Folding and manipulating paper provides practice for eye-hand coordination.

7. ***Opportunities to examine and practice spatial relationships:*** Spatial concepts include right & left, front & back, top & bottom, inside & outside, beside, under, parallel, symmetrical, etc. All of these are key components of paperfolding.

8. ***Supplemental material:*** The Bible stories can be used to complement units in basic subjects such as math, geography, history, art, music, or science.

9. ***Opportunities to enhance social skills:*** Increased self-esteem is a by-product of successfully learning new skills. Ideas for social interactions are provided in the sections for optional follow-up activities.

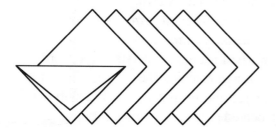

Is previous storytelling or paperfolding experience required?

No! All you need is an open mind and a fearless attitude. And a few pieces of paper…

The strength of this system is its simplicity. There are no complicated symbols or specialized terms in the directions. The illustrations were drawn so that beginners with no previous paperfolding experience can follow along with success and confidence. For storytellers who stumble over the "getting started" phase, optional introductory statements are offered with every story.

But please read the next section called, "Before you begin." It is loaded with tips based on experiences gained from the field-testing phase of this book.

Who should use Bible Folding Stories?

• ***Art teachers*** who would like to introduce origami in an educational and non-threatening way to inexperienced paperfolders.

• ***Camp leaders*** who would like to combine an inexpensive paper craft with Biblical text.

• ***Storytellers*** who enjoy new and unusual props to peak their listeners' interest.

• ***Religious educators*** who are seeking new ways to present Biblical text to their students, or are looking for ways to supplement their regular curriculums.

• ***Recreation, troop and club leaders*** who organize and present wholesome activities on limited budgets.

• ***Origami specialists*** who present workshops to novice folders and would like to introduce basic folding techniques in an interesting and effective format.

• ***Parents, grandparents, uncles & aunts*** who would like to enhance family activities with a fun and creative new hobby.

• ***Program organizers*** who are seeking material for families or groups composed of mixed ages and diverse interests.

**For best results,
follow these guidelines:**

1. Match the story activities to your group.

2. Prefold the origami figure.

3. Have required materials prepared.

4. Be familiar with the story.

5. Enhance the story with related Biblical history.

6. Plan a response to reluctant folders.

7. Expect and accept imperfect first folds.

8. Understand folding directions.

BEFORE YOU BEGIN

Match the story activities to your group.

Every story in this book features a different origami model. The stories are based on Biblical text that has been simplified so that it can be enjoyed and understood by virtually all age groups. The origami figures were selected because they are symbolic of the featured Old Testament stories and are among the easiest and least complex to learn how to fold. Success with these simple models help non-folders feel confident and comfortable with elementary paperfolding techniques. However, even with these basic models, varying levels of difficulty exist. It is important to select follow-up activities that match your group's abilities, ages, interests, and developmental levels.

It is perfectly acceptable to tell the Bible stories without teaching the origami folds, particularly if you have time constraints or your group size is too large or too young to effectively learn the folding techniques.

Prefold the origami figure for most effective storytelling.

The most pleasing origami models are constructed with clean, sharp folds where the paper edges are precisely aligned. Expert folders can accomplish this feat without the support of a hard, flat surface. But the rest of us need a flat surface to make accurate creases. Unfortunately, hard flat surfaces are not always available or practical in storytelling locations.

To overcome this presentation problem and to be able to tell the story smoothly without taking excessive folding time, it is *essential* to prefold the model featured in your selected story. Then, as you approach each step, the folds will simply snap into place. You will not fumble with the paper nor suddenly forget what to do. Your story delivery will be confident and dynamic as you concentrate on the story text and your group's responses.

Have all required materials ready before you begin.

The title page for each story includes a photograph of the featured origami model, a brief description of the story, and a list of materials required for the presentation of the story. If you plan to teach the model or use the story to support other activities, you will need several pieces of paper for each group member. Plan to have plenty of paper for practice or mistakes.

Be familiar with the text.

Experienced storytellers will want to memorize the stories for their presentations. But others will want to refer to the book as they present the stories. For this reason, the photos of the featured origami figures are placed on the title pages *only*, so that when the story is open in front of a group, the listeners will not be able to see what figure will finally emerge.

This element of surprise makes the stories more intriguing and ironic. Listeners of all ages are delighted when the final figure emerges. As always, story presentations are most effective when the storyteller is very familiar with the material.

Enhance the stories with Biblical history and personal applications.

All of the stories are very short and highlight only a limited part of the Old Testament. But they all present important and powerful messages that often motivate further exploration.

Listeners are often curious about what happened historically before and after the story occurred. They want to compare the family traditions presented in the story with those of their own families. They want to explore the possibilities of miracles. They want to confront the problems of modern starvation and famine. They want to understand the characteristics of righteousness. They want to discuss what happened to them when they prayed, or disobeyed, or caused pain. They want to feel the emotions of the stories, and to share those feelings with others. They want to compare the stories to their own lives.

Make time for these discussions before, during, or after you tell the stories. Let your presentation style and the demands of your group dictate when you introduce extended topics. Perhaps your group might be eager to fold paper. If that's all they can think about, then wait until they're finished folding to apply the lessons. But if there are burning questions during the storytelling, take time to respond to them then.

The stories work perfectly as supplements to regular curriculums, but they also fit neatly into a wide variety of subject areas or units of study. The skills and subjects addressed by the optional follow-up activities are listed and cross-referenced in the index.

Not all of the activities are appropriate for all groups and are not designed to be presented together. They are merely suggestions for the storyteller or are intended to spark a new idea for a creative use for the story or its resulting origami model.

Areas have been designated in these sections for noting when you used the stories, which activities you included, and what responses you received. It is often helpful to log presentation details so that future planning can be facilitated.

Plan a response for reluctant folders.

Some children and adults are so afraid of ruining the paper, making mistakes, or attempting new activities that they won't even try. They exclaim loudly, "I *can't* do it!"

One way to overcome this reluctance is to avoid distributing practice paper until the story is finished and the folding sequence has been reviewed. This helps the group feel confident about remembering what comes next and eliminates worry related to forgetfulness.

Discourage participants from folding along as you first tell the story. This distracts other group members and reduces the folder's ability to associate the story events with the progressive folding steps. Learning would therefore be less effective.

Fold the first attempt together as a group, saying often, "Yes! That's right. This is easy." Affirming that the task is not hard and publicly praising successful efforts sets a positive tone for beginners. Ask group members who are seated next to reluctant folders to show them how they did it, offering assistance without folding it for them.

Always relate the folding steps to the story events, reinforcing the associations so that

memory is enhanced. When a folder can not remember what step comes next, instead of simply telling him, ask, "What did the ark need on top to keep out the rain?" or "How many stars were in Joseph's dream?" When these associations between the story and the folds are emphasized, long term memory is improved.

Reluctant folders are often reassured when a casual or humorous presentation style is used. Be excited. Act amazed. Smile. Too much perfection or seriousness promotes folding reluctance and fear of failure.

Expect and accept imperfect folds from beginners.

New paperfolders sometimes feel overwhelmed by the experience, especially if they have a dependent learning style. During the first folding trial, emphasize the sequence of steps necessary to create the model, rather than the precision of their efforts. Regardless of how inaccurate first attempts may appear, most beginners are pleased with their results and surprised that paperfolding really is easy. They immediately want to make another one.

During second and third attempts, begin to emphasize the quality and sharpness of the folds, suggesting that the model will be more attractive when all of the edges and corners are lined up exactly during every step. Encourage them to slow down. As beginning folders become more confident, give them smaller and smaller squares of paper to fold. This increases precision and sustains an element of surprise or challenge throughout the practicing phase.

Avoid criticizing lop-sided or ragged first results. Instead, say, "Yes! I *knew* you could do it! Let's make another one to share. This time, try lining up the edges before you crease the paper. That might help it stand up better."

How to make the origami figures:

1. Every story includes a summary of folding directions. Use these directions when prefolding the origami figure. Then go back to see where the folds occur in the story. Always use a prefolded model to tell the stories. (Simply unfold the completed model so that all the necessary creases will already be there.)

2. Most of figures in this book, except those folded with newspaper, start as squares. It is important that the squares be exactly the same length on all sides. Squares can easily be made from rectangular paper by folding a corner down (as shown) and trimming away the excess:

3. Origami paper can be purchased pre-cut in a variety of beautiful colors and textures. However, all of the figures in this book can be made very successfully with paper you already have in your home, office or classroom. Experiment with different weights and textures for the most satisfying results.

4. Use a hard, flat surface when making initial folds. Line up edges and corners precisely and hold in place before you crease.

5. Follow each step in the directions in the order they are given. Only after you are very proficient in making a figure, should you attempt to alter the established technique.

6. Explanation of symbols:

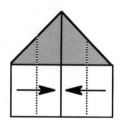

Shaded areas indicate that the back side of the paper is now facing up.

Arrows point to the direction of the fold.

Dotted or dashed lines mark where the next crease will be.

Solid lines indicate existing creases, folds, or edges.

Scissors are used to make this lovely dove from traditional square paper, rectangles, or from a round paper plate. Folding directions are summarized on page 17.

About the story:

Noah and his family build an ark and fill it with animals and food. They are protected from the flood that destroys the rest of the world. They know it is safe to come out when their dove does not return to them. *Based on Genesis 6 - 9:15.*

Recommended ages:

Listening only: age 4 through adult.
Listening and paperfolding: age 5 through adult.

Required materials:

Scissors and one square of paper at least eight inches on each side, folded through Fold #3, and then completely unfolded for storytelling. *Do not cut the wings ahead of time.*

Optional introductory statement:

"I'm going to tell you the story of how a good man and his family survived a terrible flood. Watch carefully as I fold paper into different shapes. This is called origami, or Japanese paperfolding. The name of the story is…"

Noah's Ark *Genesis 6 - 9:15*

A long, long, long time ago, when the world was still quite new, the Lord saw that there was much wickedness on Earth. The people living on Earth in those days were not good like we are. The people living on Earth a long, long time ago had bad ideas and they did mean, violent things to hurt each other.

When God saw how badly they behaved, he was broken-hearted. God said, "I will blot out man whom I have created, man and beast and creeping things and birds of the air, for I am sorry that I have made them."

But then God saw that there was one kind and righteous man on Earth. Noah and his family were good. They were worth saving, for they did kind and helpful things for others. So God told them to build a waterproof wooden ark that would float while flood waters destroyed the other evil things on Earth.

Noah and his family built the boat just as God instructed. It was very large with three decks inside. *(Hold up Fold #1 as the bottom of the ark and indicate where three decks might be.)*

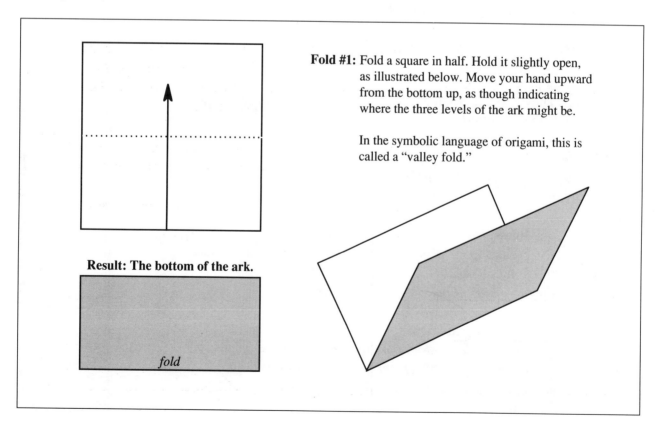

Fold #1: Fold a square in half. Hold it slightly open, as illustrated below. Move your hand upward from the bottom up, as though indicating where the three levels of the ark might be.

In the symbolic language of origami, this is called a "valley fold."

Result: The bottom of the ark.

fold

Fold #2: Open the rectangle formed in Fold #1 so that the crease forms a vertical midline. Fold the top to the middle and crease along the dotted lines as shown to the right.

In the symbolic language of origami, this is called a "mountain fold."

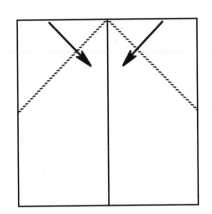

Result: The roof of the ark.

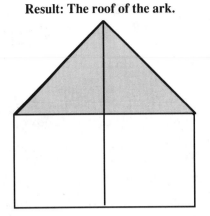

There was a roof on top *(demonstrate with Fold #2)* and a door along the side. God told Noah to gather a male and female of every type of animal on Earth so that they could also be protected from the flood. The Lord said, "Also take with you every sort of food that is eaten, and store it up; and it shall serve as food for you and for them."

Noah and his wife, their three sons and their wives, and all of the animals went into the ark and <u>shut the door</u>. *(Demonstrate with Fold #3.)* <u>The sky</u> *(use Fold #3 to point upward to the sky)* darkened and the rain began to fall.

It rained for forty days and forty nights. The flood waters rose and the ark floated. The flood lasted for 150 days. Then God made a wind blow over the earth and the water began to dry up. Finally the ark came to rest on the mountains of Ararat. *(Turn Fold #3 as shown and point to the slope to represent Mount Ararat.)*

Fold #3: On the words, "shut the door," fold the figure in half along its vertical midline. On the words, "the sky," point upward with the figure. Then turn it as shown and point to the slope which represents Mount Ararat.

Result: Mount Ararat.

Point to this slope.

After forty days of waiting on Mount Ararat, Noah opened the window of the ark *(demonstrate by opening the cut flaps of Fold #4)* and sent out a raven. The raven flew around and around but could not find a place to land.

Then Noah sent out a dove. *(Demonstrate with Fold #5, the complete dove.)*

The dove also flew around and around, and when it could not find a dry place to rest, it returned to the ark. Noah waited seven days before releasing the dove again. This time, it returned with an olive leaf in its beak, a sign that the earth was getting drier. Noah waited seven more days before letting the dove make a third attempt at finding dry land. This third time, the dove did not come back. It had finally found a dry place to live. The flood was over.

Noah removed the covering from the ark and saw that the ground was dry. God told him to leave the ark and release the animals, so that they could all live on the earth again. Noah obeyed, and built an altar to the Lord to give thanks. And then the Lord promised that never again shall there be a flood to destroy the earth.

God said, "My rainbow in the clouds shall be a sign of the promise between me and the earth. When the rainbow is seen in the clouds, I will remember my promise and the waters shall never again become a flood to destroy the earth."

So from that day until now, a rainbow is not only beautiful, but it is also a reminder of God's promise to us.

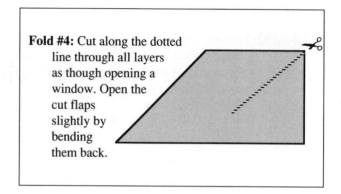

Fold #4: Cut along the dotted line through all layers as though opening a window. Open the cut flaps slightly by bending them back.

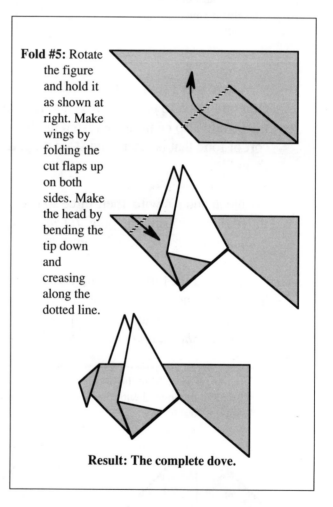

Fold #5: Rotate the figure and hold it as shown at right. Make wings by folding the cut flaps up on both sides. Make the head by bending the tip down and creasing along the dotted line.

Result: The complete dove.

Summary of folding directions

Fold #1: Fold a square in half, then unfold it for the next step.

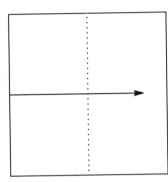

Fold #2: Open the rectangle formed in Fold #1 so that the crease forms a vertical midline. Fold the top to the middle and crease along the dotted lines.

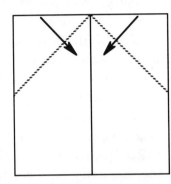

Fold #3: Fold the figure in half along its vertical midline, then rotate it as shown.

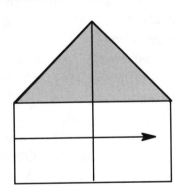
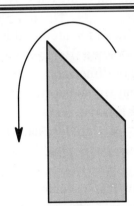

Fold #4: Cut along the dotted line through all layers.

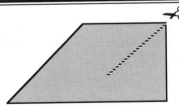

Fold #5: Rotate the figure and hold as shown to the far right. Make wings by folding the cut flaps up on both sides. Make the head by bending the tip down and creasing along the dotted line.

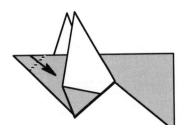
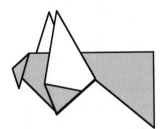

Result: The complete dove.

Optional follow-up activities for "Noah's Ark"

1. After telling the story, review the sequence of folds used to construct a dove. Emphasize the correct order, giving each step its name from the story: ark bottom, ark roof, Mount Ararat, opening the window, and finally, the dove. With a fresh, unfolded piece of paper, reconstruct the dove for your group, asking them to identify each step and tell you what comes next. As you fold the dove, emphasize how to line up the edges before creasing firmly. Distribute paper and scissors *only* after your group is confident about the folding procedure. Then fold the first dove together as a group, step by step, identifying each step by its name from the story.

2. The dove featured in this story can also be constructed from rectangles or circles of any size or dimension. After the folding sequence is learned, experiment with papers of different sizes and textures, following the same folding procedure each time. A dove folded from a paper plate is shown on page 13.

3. Draw feathery markings on a finished dove. Then make the same designs on another, unfolded piece of paper. Fold the decorated paper into a dove. Compare it to the first dove that was decorated after it was folded. Observe differences and similarities. Is it better to decorate paper before it is folded, or when the figure is complete?

4. Make doves as gifts or as peace offerings. Include a simulated olive branch (olive leaves are dark green, narrow, and stiff) or a sprig of natural greenery.

5. Display your group's doves on a bulletin board with a multicolored rainbow background, combine them to make a group mobile, dangle them separately from the ceiling, or hang them on a tree.

6. Ask, "If you had to suddenly leave your home in an emergency, what would you take with you?"

7. Use the story to introduce or complement discussions or lessons about:
   a. Righteousness - what characteristics made Noah righteous?
   b. Floods - personal experiences with.
   c. Obedience.
   d. Animals.
   e. Rainbows.
   f. Starting over with a clean slate.
   g. Noah's descendents - the generations of his sons, Shem, Ham, and Japheth and the nations they began.

Date	Group	Notes

This charming infant is wrapped snugly in its paper blanket. Above, a face is added for greater reality. Folding directions are summarized on page 23.

About the story:
Abraham and Sarah are blessed with a baby in their old age. *Based on Genesis 15:1 - 5, 17:16, and 21:1 - 6.*

Recommended ages:
Listening only: age 4 through adult.
Listening and paperfolding: age 7 through adult.

Required materials:
One square of paper at least eight inches on each side, folded into a baby, and then completely unfolded for storytelling.

Optional introductory statement:
"I'm going to tell you the story of how Abraham and Sarah become parents in their old age. Watch carefully as I fold paper into different shapes. This is called origami, or Japanese paperfolding. The name of the story is…"

Sarah, Mother of Nations *Genesis 15: 1 - 5, 17: 16, 21: 1 - 6*

Many, many years ago, a man named Abram and his wife, Sarai, were very old. Their lives were exciting and important. During their long years together, they journeyed over deserts *(hold the paper flat to represent a desert)…*

They crossed rivers great and small. *(Demonstrate with Fold #1, holding it open to represent a river.)*

And they climbed through many mountains. *(Close Fold #1 and hold it up to represent a mountain.)*

But throughout all these adventures and explorations, they had no children.

Once, while Abram was feeling sad about not having children, the Lord came to him in a vision.

God said, "Look toward heaven *(hold Fold #2 as though it were an arrow pointing up to the sky)* and count the stars if you can. That is how many children will one day be born into your family."

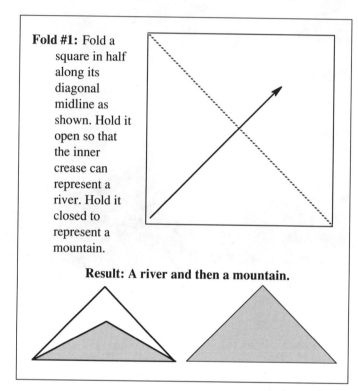

Fold #1: Fold a square in half along its diagonal midline as shown. Hold it open so that the inner crease can represent a river. Hold it closed to represent a mountain.

Result: A river and then a mountain.

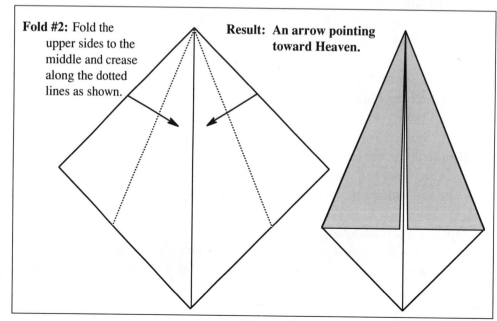

Fold #2: Fold the upper sides to the middle and crease along the dotted lines as shown.

Result: An arrow pointing toward Heaven.

20

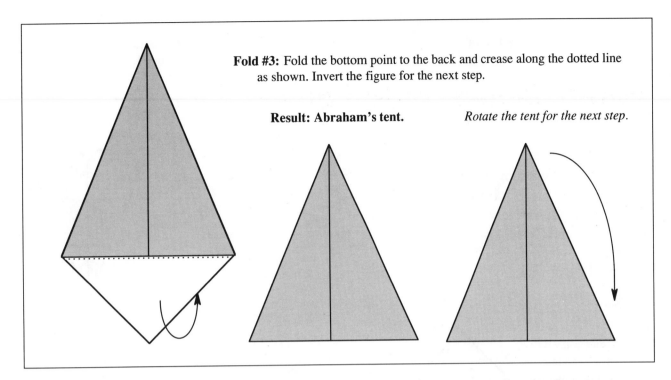

Fold #3: Fold the bottom point to the back and crease along the dotted line as shown. Invert the figure for the next step.

Result: Abraham's tent.

Rotate the tent for the next step.

When Abram was ninety-nine years old and living in a tent *(hold up Fold #3)*, God came to him again and said, "I am God almighty. I will make a promise between me and you. You shall be the father of many nations. No longer shall your name be Abram, but now your name shall be Abraham. I will bless your wife, Sarai, and give you a son through her. Her name shall now be Sarah and she shall be a mother of nations; kings of peoples shall come from her."

Sarah was ninety years old. She laughed, thinking that she was too old to ever be able to <u>wrap her own child</u> in a blanket like this *(demonstrate with Fold #4)*.

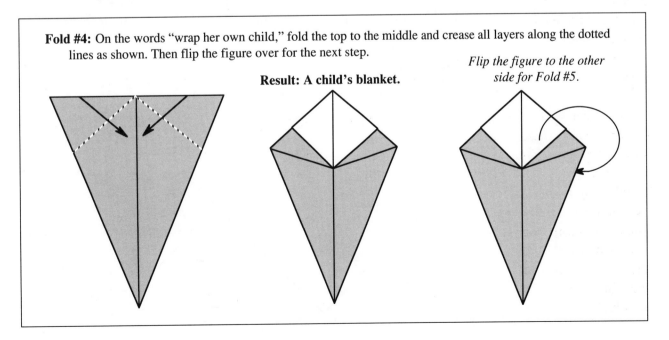

Fold #4: On the words "wrap her own child," fold the top to the middle and crease all layers along the dotted lines as shown. Then flip the figure over for the next step.

Result: A child's blanket.

Flip the figure to the other side for Fold #5.

But the Lord visited Sarah as he had said, and Sarah did have a baby to cuddle and care for. *(Demonstrate with Folds #5 and #6, the complete swaddled baby.)*

Abraham was one hundred years old when his son, Isaac, was born. Sarah was very happy. She said, "God has given me laughter; and all who hear, will laugh with me."

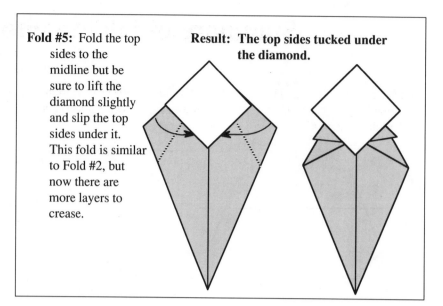

Fold #5: Fold the top sides to the midline but be sure to lift the diamond slightly and slip the top sides under it. This fold is similar to Fold #2, but now there are more layers to crease.

Result: The top sides tucked under the diamond.

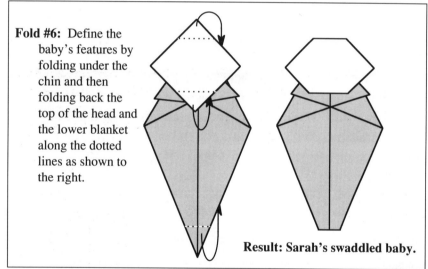

Fold #6: Define the baby's features by folding under the chin and then folding back the top of the head and the lower blanket along the dotted lines as shown to the right.

Result: Sarah's swaddled baby.

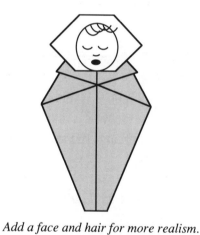

Add a face and hair for more realism.

Summary of folding directions

Fold #1: Fold a square in half along its diagonal midline. Unfold for Fold #2.

Fold #2: Fold the lower sides to the middle and crease along the dotted lines.

Fold #3: Fold the top point to the back and crease along the dotted line.

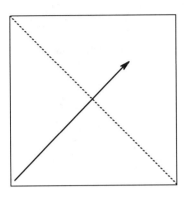

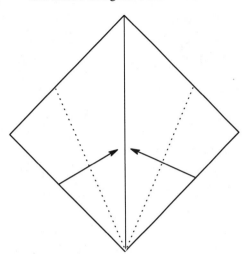

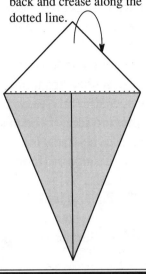

Fold #4: Fold the top to the middle and crease all layers along the dotted lines. Then flip the figure over for Fold #5.

Fold #5: Fold the top sides to the midline but be sure to lift the diamond slightly and slip the top sides under it. This fold is similar to Fold #2, but now there are more layers to crease.

Result

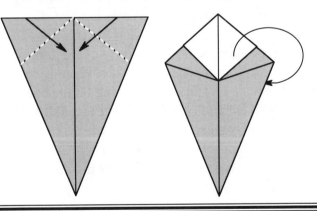

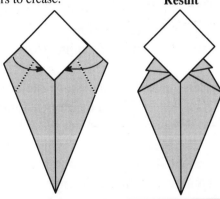

Fold #6: Define the baby's features by folding under the chin and then folding back the top of the head and the lower blanket along the dotted lines.

Result: A swaddled baby.

Optional follow-up activities for "Sarah, Mother of Nations"

1. After telling the story, review the sequence of folds used to construct the baby. Emphasize the correct order, giving each step its name from the story: mountain, arrow, tent, etc. With a fresh, unfolded piece of paper, reconstruct the baby for your group, asking them to identify each step and tell you what comes next. If group members can't remember the next step, offer them a hint by referring back to the story: "Where did God tell Abraham to look to see how many children would be born into his family? Yes, up. Let's fold the upper sides like this…"

   Emphasize the need to slowly line up the edges, pressing the creases firmly and completely. Distribute paper *only* after your group is confident about the folding procedure. Then fold the first baby together as a group, step by step, continuing to identify each step by its name from the story.

2. The baby featured in this story can be made any size, depending on the dimensions of the square you begin with. After the folding sequence is learned, experiment with papers of different sizes, following the same folding procedure each time. Challenge your group to determine the ratio of starting size to finished size. If a 8.5 inch square yields a 6 inch baby, what size baby will a 12 inch square make? *(answer: 8.47)* Fold a 12 inch square into a baby to validate your answer.

3. Add faces and hair to finished babies and decorate the blankets. Predict where the markings will be when the babies are unfolded. Unfold to test your prediction. Are the markings scattered? Are they all on the same side of the paper? Do the faces still look like faces? Refold the babies and watch the faces and blanket decorations pop back into place.

4. Punch a hole in the top of the decorated babies, lace with yarn, and use as name tags, book markers, or necklaces.

5. Represent the night sky by stapling dark blue construction paper to a bulletin board. Post Genesis 15:5 in large lettering on the board. Then ask each group member to add his or her origami baby to the display, symbolizing Abraham's descendants. Finish by adding stars to represent descendants that haven't yet been born.

Date	Group	Notes

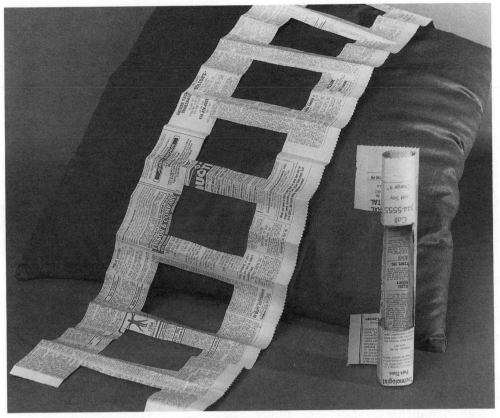

Surprise your listeners when this newspaper ladder suddenly appears!

About the story:
Jacob falls asleep on a stone pillow and dreams about a ladder stretching between Heaven and Earth. *Based on Genesis 28:1 - 22.*

Recommended ages:
Listening and paperfolding: age 4 through adult.

Required materials:
A strip of newspaper eight inches wide and 27 inches long.
Scissors.

Optional introductory statement:
"I'm going to tell you the story of how Jacob dreamed about the house of God. Watch very carefully during the story, because I'm going to show you how to do a newspaper trick . The name of the story is…"

Jacob's Ladder *Genesis 28:1 - 22*

Isaac, Abraham and Sarah's son, was concerned about who his son Jacob would marry. Like his father before him, Isaac wanted Jacob to marry just the right woman. So Isaac sent his son, Jacob, on a journey from Beer-sheba to another land called Haran in order to find a proper wife. Jacob obeyed his father and prepared for his trip by gathering up his belongings like this. *(Gather up the eight inch wide newspaper as in Step #1.)*

By the time Jacob reached a certain place in the hill country north of Jerusalem, it was dark and he was tired. He decided to spend the night. He took a stone *(cut out the rectangle through all thicknesses as indicated in Step #2 and wad it up to represent the stone)* and used it for a pillow as he lay down to sleep.

While he was sleeping, Jacob had a wonderful dream. He dreamed that there was a ladder set up on the earth and the top of it reached to heaven. *(Hold onto the loose ends of Step #3 and jerk the paper, causing the paper to suddenly unroll into a ladder.)*

On the ladder, he saw angels climbing up and down. God stood next to Jacob and said, "I am the Lord, the God of Abraham your father and the God of Isaac. The land on which you

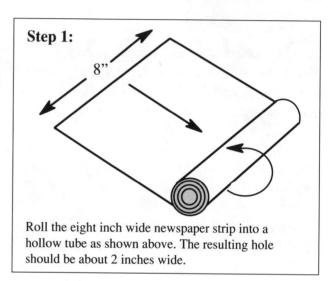

Step 1:

8"

Roll the eight inch wide newspaper strip into a hollow tube as shown above. The resulting hole should be about 2 inches wide.

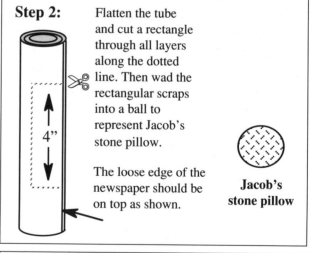

Step 2: Flatten the tube and cut a rectangle through all layers along the dotted line. Then wad the rectangular scraps into a ball to represent Jacob's stone pillow.

4"

The loose edge of the newspaper should be on top as shown.

Jacob's stone pillow

Step 3: Hold the figure by the loose ends and let it unroll into a ladder.

lie, I will give to you and to your descendants; and your descendants shall be like the dust of the earth and you shall spread abroad to the west and to the east and to the north and to the south; and through you and your descendants shall all the families of the earth be blessed. Behold, I am with you and will keep you wherever you go, and will not leave you until I have done that which I have spoken to you."

Then Jacob woke up from his sleep feeling afraid. He said, "Surely the Lord is in this place and I did not know it. This is none other than the house of God, and this is the gate of heaven."

Early the next morning, Jacob made a pillar, or monument, from the stone that had been his pillow. *(Roll the stone pillow into a pillar.)*

He poured oil on it and named the place "Bethel", which means "house of God." Then Jacob made a promise, saying, "If God will be with me and keep me wherever I go, and give me bread to eat and clothes to wear, so that I may come again to my father's house in peace, then the Lord shall be my God; and this stone, which I have set up as a pillar, shall be God's house; and of all that you give me I will surely give a tenth back to you."

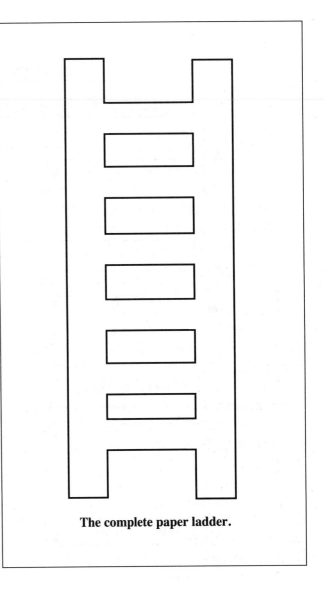

The complete paper ladder.

Jacob's Ladder

adaption of an African American folksong

2. Every round goes higher, higher, etc.
3. If you love Him, you must serve Him, etc.
4. We are climbing higher, higher, etc.
5. *repeat the first verse*

Optional follow-up activities for "Jacob's Ladder"

1. After the story is told, distribute newspaper sections for cutting and rolling (if your time, space, or number of scissors is limited, pre-cut the newspaper before distribution). For best results, be sure that the loose edge of the newspaper is aligned with the side of the flattened roll before cutting the rectangle. Try unrolling all the ladders simultaneously as a group or one at a time in rapid succession. Ladders can always be re-rolled by simply matching up the sides and rungs created by the rectangular cut.

2. Color the newspaper before rolling. Wait until the ladder has been cut before applying pasted or glued symbols or decorations.

3. If you stand the dove from "Noah's Ark" (see page 17) on its tail, it resembles the form of an angel. Adjust its "beak" to appear more like a face. Construct several out of small paper (four inch squares or smaller) and staple to the decorated ladders. Display on one large bulletin board or dangle all of the ladders from the ceiling.

4. Use a large map during or after storytelling to point to Beer-sheba (where Jacob was living with Isaac), Bethel (north of Beer-sheba where Jacob dreamed of the ladder), and Haran in Paddan-aram (where Jacob later married Leah and Rachel).

5. Experiment with various papers and sizes. Shorter ladders can be made by rolling a strip that measures three inches wide and 14 inches long, cut easily from legal-sized copy paper. Miniature ladders can be made from strips that are two inches wide and 11.5 inches long. Your students will enjoy the challenge of creating ever smaller ladders and attaching tiny angels that are folded from one inch squares.

6. Sing the spiritual folksong, "Jacob's Ladder." Accompany with guitar and/or autoharp. (Chords are indicated with the melody and text.) Use body sounds or rhythm instruments to simulate steady footsteps. Add syncopation for an energetic undercurrent of rhythm. Ask for volunteers to sing the first four measures of each verse as a solo, with the rest of the group joining on measure five. Use the paper ladders as props, unrolling them simultaneously and dramatically on the last verse. Perform for another group or videotape for later viewing.

7. Emphasize cooperation by combining all the group's rectangular scraps into one "stone pillow." Use it to re-enact the construction of the pillar at Bethel, reciting Jacob's promise to God. Relate to the practice of tithing (tithe is one tenth). Research and discuss other Biblical references to tithing.

8. God told Jacob that He was with him and would "keep" him. Ask your group members if they are aware of God's presence in their lives. Encourage discussion and sharing.

9. A twisted ladder can be made by altering the unrolling procedure. Instead of simply releasing the ladder, stand the two side rolls side by side, with the ladder rungs forming a bridge between them, as illustrated below.

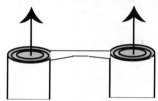

To form the ladder, pull up the innermost coil, so that tight spirals rise up on each side. This procedure is similar to the formation of the spike of wheat in the story about Ruth and Naomi, found on page 47.

10. Use the story to introduce or complement discussions or lessons about:

a. Jacob's experiences in Haran and the historical significance of his twelve sons.
b. Jacob's many other accomplishments.
c. Jacob's name change to Israel.
d. The significance of "dreams" in the Bible.
e. Jacob's dreams as compared to Joseph's dreams.
f. The importance of angels in the Book of Genesis.
g. Family traditions and laws in Genesis.
h. The concept of having a guardian angel.
i. Abraham's descendents.

Date	Group	Notes

This traditional robe can easily be made into a puppet by adding a face as shown above. Folding directions are summarized on page 36.

About the story:

Joseph's angry and envious brothers sell him to slave traders on their way to Egypt. Unwilling to tell their father what they have done to his favorite son, the brothers dip Joseph's robe in blood and pretend that he was eaten by wild animals. *Based on Genesis 37:1 - 34, 45:4 - 5. 50:20 - 22*

Recommended ages:

Listening only: age 4 through adult.
Listening and paperfolding: age 6 through adult.

Required materials:

A square of plain or striped paper at least eight inches on each side, folded into a robe and then completely unfolded for storytelling.

Optional introductory statement:

"I'm going to tell you a story of how something bad turned out to be a part of God's plan to do something good. Watch carefully as I fold this paper into different shapes. This is called origami, or Japanese paperfolding. The name of the story is..."

JOSEPH'S DREAMS COME TRUE

Joseph's Dreams Come True

Genesis 37:1 - 34, 45:4 - 5, 50:20 - 22

Before you begin: Fold a square in half. Then fold it in half again. Unfold for storytelling. The creases divide the paper into four equal squares. The center of the square is located where the two lines meet. In origami, this preparatory step is called a preliminary fold. It provides necessary guidelines for well-balanced paperfolding.

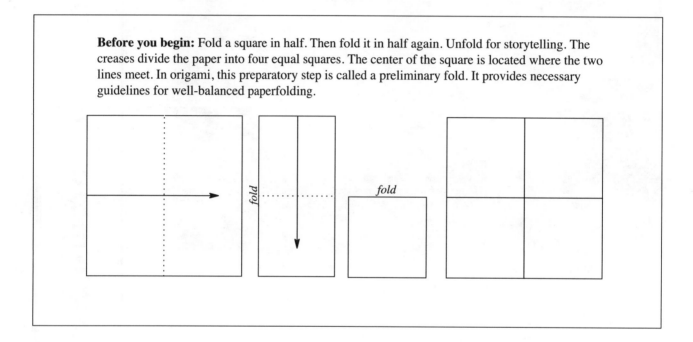

A man named Jacob, who was the grandson of Abraham, lived in the land of Canaan. He had twelve sons, but his favorite son was Joseph because Joseph was born when Jacob was an old man. Joseph helped his older brothers take care of the family's sheep. Sometimes Joseph would tell his father about his brothers' mistakes, and this caused his brothers to mistrust and dislike him.

The brothers also felt jealous about the way that Jacob, their father, loved Joseph more than any of them. They were especially angry when their father gave Joseph a splendid long-sleeved robe of many colors that was much better than the robes they had to wear. They felt so angry that they would not speak kindly to Joseph at all.

One night, Joseph had a vivid dream. He dreamed that all the brothers were tying up bundles of wheat in the field. All of a sudden, Joseph's bundle stood up straight while all of his brothers' bundles bowed down before it.

"Does that mean," they asked, "that you are more important than us? Do we have to bow down to you?"

They didn't like that idea at all.

Another time, Joseph dreamed that the sun and the moon (*pause while you fold the first corner to represent the sun and the moon*) and eleven stars bowed down to him.

Fold the next eleven corners as you count the eleven stars:

One…

Two…

Three…

Flip the figure here.

Four…

Five…

Six…

Seven…

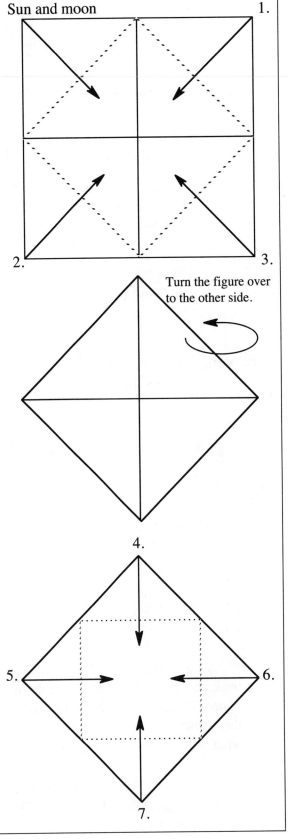

Sun and moon

Fold the corners to the middle point that was created in the preliminary folds. Flip the figure over, and repeat. After each of the four corners are folded in, flip over to the other side. There will be a total of twelve corners folded all together. Be sure to press firmly. The figure will be quite bulky by the time the last corners are folded to the center.

Let the first corner represent the "sun and the moon" while the other eleven corners each represent one of the stars in Joseph's dream. Say the number as you fold the corner.

Turn the figure over to the other side.

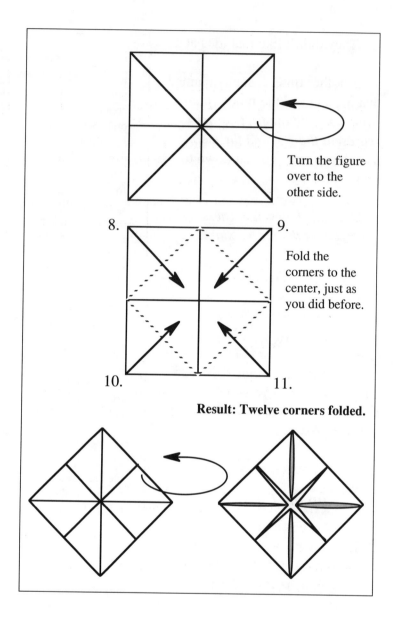

Flip the figure here.

Eight…

Nine…

Ten…

Eleven… stars all bowed down before him.

Flip the figure for the final time.

Turn the figure over to the other side.

8. 9.

Fold the corners to the center, just as you did before.

10. 11.

Result: Twelve corners folded.

Even his father, Jacob, was surprised about this dream. He asked, "Are you trying to tell me that this dream means that your parents and your brothers will all bow down to you some day?"

A short while later, Jacob sent Joseph out to find his brothers so that he could report back about how the sheep were doing. When the brothers saw Joseph coming, they planned to hurt him. They said, "Look, here comes the dreamer. Let us beat him up and throw him into a pit. We will say that an evil beast has eaten him, and then we shall see what will become of his dreams."

But the oldest brother, Reuben, convinced the others not to hurt him. Instead, they pulled, and pulled, and pulled. Then they pushed and pushed (*demonstrate with the last steps in making the complete robe*) until they stripped off Joseph's special long-sleeved robe and tossed him down into an empty pit.

Reuben had secretly planned to rescue Joseph and return him to Jacob. But first, he had to go out and check on the sheep. While Reuben was away, the other brothers saw a group of traders passing by. They decided that it would not be right to harm their own brother, and that it would be better to sell Joseph as a slave. Reuben was very upset when he returned and discovered that Joseph was gone.

The brothers were unwilling to tell their father, Jacob, the truth about what they had done to Joseph. They knew he would be very angry. So they killed a goat and dipped Joseph's robe in the blood. They brought it to their father who recognized it and cried out, "It is my son's robe. An evil beast must have devoured him! Joseph has without doubt been torn in pieces!"

But of course, Joseph had not been eaten by an evil beast. He was taken to Egypt where he eventually became a wise and powerful ruler. Years later, when there was a famine and the brothers were seeking food in Egypt, they came and bowed down before Pharaoh's chief officer. Joseph's dream had come true!

He told them, "I am your brother Joseph, who you sold into Egypt."

Joseph then sent his brothers to bring their father, Jacob, to Egypt so that they could be together again. Jacob came, and later, after he died, Joseph forgave his brothers, saying, "You meant evil against me, but God meant if for good. Do not be afraid. I will take care of you and your families."

Joseph kept his promise, and Hebrew families stayed and lived in Egypt for many, many years to come.

On the repeated words, "pulled," pull the lower flap down, then pull the right and left flaps out. As you pull them, open them slightly so that little rectangles are formed.

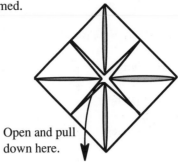

Open and pull down here.

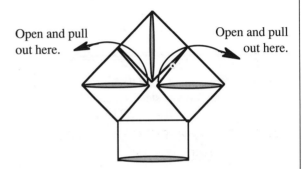

Open and pull out here.

Open and pull out here.

Next, on the repeated words, "pushed," push the right and left side corners to the inside of the sleeve. Separate the top section slightly to form a hood.

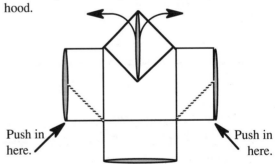

Push in here.

Push in here.

Result: Joseph's special long-sleeved robe.

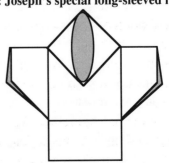

35

Summary of folding directions

Preliminary Folds: Fold a square in half. Then fold it in half again. Unfold for the next step. The creases divide the paper into four equal squares. The center of the square is located where the two lines meet.

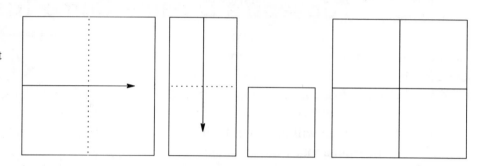

Fold the four corners to the middle point that was created in the preliminary folds, then flip the figure over. Do this "four corner folding and flipping step" a total of three times. Don't forget to flip after the twelfth corner has been folded. Be sure to press firmly. The figure will be small and quite bulky by the time the last corners are folded to the center.

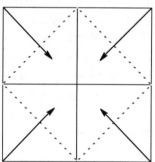 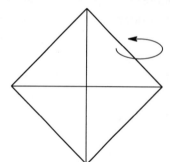

Result: Twelve corners folded.

Pull the lower flap down, then pull the right and left flaps out. As you pull them, open them slightly so that little rectangles are formed.

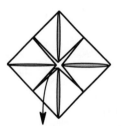 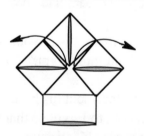

Result: A long-sleeved robe.

Next, push the right and left side corners to the inside of the sleeve. Separate the top section slightly to form a hood.

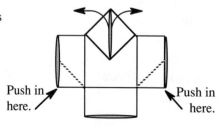

Push in here.   Push in here.

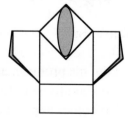

Optional follow-up activities for "Joseph's Dreams Come True"

1. After the story is told, pull the robe apart and reconstruct it for your group, being careful to identify the steps according to their names in the story: the sun and the moon, the eleven stars, and finally the pushing and pulling to make a complete robe. Fold it again with fresh, unfolded paper to demonstrate how to crease thoroughly and precisely. This time, ask your group to be the teachers and tell you the folding steps. When they say the steps in unison, their auditory memory is reinforced. Emphasize and exaggerate the "flipping" step, for this is the part that beginners often forget. It may be helpful to establish a rhythmic pattern by chanting:

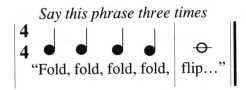

Say this phrase three times

"Fold, fold, fold, fold, flip…"

Distribute practice paper and fold the first robe together as a group.

2. Decorate paper squares before folding. Use vivid colors to simulate brightly striped fabric. Be careful to place the colored side face down when starting with the first step. Next, decorate a plain, finished robe, then unfold it and analyze where the markings are on the flat paper. Put it back together and observe the decorative markings fall back into place. Decide if it's better to decorate before folding or afterwards.

3. Finished robes can easily be converted into "people" puppets, as illustrated below. Break a popsicle stick in half. Tape each section inside the sleeves to form arms. Next, attach a full popsicle stick inside the bottom section. You may substitute paper hands for the arms. Simply cut them out and tape in place. Gluing or pasting is not recommended because the sleeves could inadvertently become sealed. Draw facial features and clothes. Include characteristics of the person you wish to simulate. A puppet with an open hood is created by inserting a face, or by drawing the facial features on the layer of paper beneath the hood. Use yarn or cotton for hair or beards. For characters who wore garments with shorter sleeves (Joseph's brothers), simply fold up the sleeves in the same manner as you would shorten any

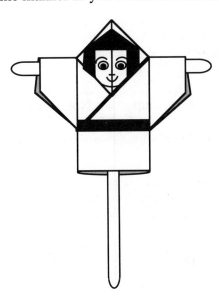

sleeve. Make adult puppets from larger squares (and children from smaller squares), without altering the folding procedure.

4. Ask different group members to make a puppet character from the story. Include Jacob, the sons of Leah (Reuben, Simeon, Levi, Judah, Is'sachar), the sons of Rachel (Joseph and Benjamin), the son's of Bilhah, Rachel's maid (Dan and Naph'tali), and the sons of Zilpah, Leah's maid (Gad and Asher). Also make a group of slave traders. Ask each group member to write a short paragraph about his or her character, including details about their accomplishments and/or significance. Create a puppet stage by draping fabric or paper over a large box or table. Add appropriate props.

When the puppets and paragraphs are ready, give each puppet character a chance to tell his life story. For example, the Jacob puppet might come out and say, "Hello. God changed my name to Israel, but I was once called Jacob. My father was Isaac and my grandfather was Abraham. My mother

was…" After each puppet has a chance to introduce itself, dramatize the story, adding appropriate lines of dialog. Present for another group or videotape for later viewing.

5. It was God's will that Joseph be sent to Egypt. An evil event turned out to be good. Challenge your group members to find other examples from the Bible, history, or their personal lives of bad things that turned out to be good.

6. Use the story to introduce or complement discussions or lessons about:
   a. Jealousy.
   b. Violence.
   c. Deception.
   d. Anger.
   e. Guilt.
   f. Love/hate relationships.
   g. Forgiveness.
   h. Favoritism.
   i. Sibling rivalry.
   j. Dreams and their significance in Genesis.
   k. The historical importance of the Hebrews living in Egypt.

Date	Group	Notes

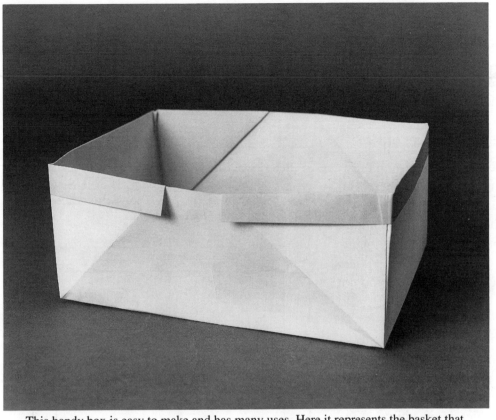

This handy box is easy to make and has many uses. Here it represents the basket that protected baby Moses along the Nile River. Folding directions are summarized on page 43.

About the story:

Pharaoh decrees that all infant sons born to Hebrew slaves must be drown in the Nile River, but a home-made basket helps to save an important little baby. *Based on Exodus 1:1 - 2:10.*

Recommended ages:

Listening only: age 4 through adult.
Listening and paperfolding: age 6 through adult.

Required materials:

A rectangle the size of copy paper (8.5" x 11") folded into the basket and then completely unfolded for storytelling.

Optional introductory statement:

"I'm going to tell you the story of how two women unknowingly worked together to save a very important baby. Watch carefully as I fold paper into different shapes. This is called origami, or Japanese paperfolding. The name of the story is…"

Baby In A Basket *Exodus 1:1 - 2:10*

When Joseph and his brothers and their families first moved to Egypt, there were only seventy Hebrews living and working there. But after four hundred years of having children who had more children, who had even more children, there were several thousand Hebrews living in Egypt. Hebrews believed in God, but Egyptians practiced a different religion. Egyptians did not believe in God.

A new Egyptian king, Pharaoh, suddenly became worried that there were too many Hebrews in Egypt. He was afraid that the Hebrews had become too powerful and might some day side with Egyptian enemies against him.

Pharaoh decided to force the Hebrews to become slaves. He made them work harder than ever making bricks and taking care of the crops in the fields. *(Hold up a rectangle to represent the fields, as shown to the right.)*

Pharaoh ordered the Hebrews to build more and more storage buildings that had great double doors like this. *(Open and close the doors represented in Fold #1.)*

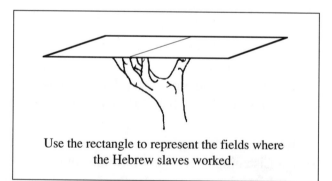

Before you begin: Fold a rectangle in half along the dotted line as shown below. Then unfold for storytelling. This preparatory step is called a preliminary fold in origami.

11"

8.5"

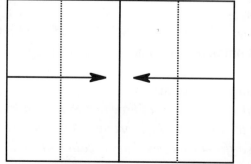

Use the rectangle to represent the fields where the Hebrew slaves worked.

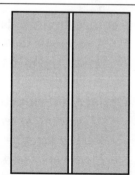

Fold #1: Fold the right and left sides to the middle crease that was created in the preliminary fold. Press firmly along the dotted lines.

Result: Great double doors

Swing the doors open and closed.

Despite the hardship that the Hebrew slaves suffered, they still flourished and did well. They continued to pray and have more children. As they grew stronger, Pharaoh felt even more afraid. He decided that the only way to weaken the Hebrews, was to drown all of their newborn sons in the Nile River, one of the largest rivers in the world.

(Point to the center section of Fold #2 to represent the Nile River.)

During this dangerous time, a Hebrew boy was born. His mother loved him and kept him hidden from Pharaoh's soldiers for three months. But as he grew bigger and stronger, the baby's cries became too loud to keep him a secret in the house any more. The baby's mother made a basket *(crease the four corners of Fold #3)*, carefully using just the right materials so that no water would leak into it.

She wrapped the baby boy warmly like this. *(Demonstrate with the wrapping motions of Fold #4.)*

Now the baby was ready to be placed gently into <u>the basket</u>.

(On the words, "the basket," open Fold #5.)

The baby's mother put the basket next to the Nile River, so

Fold #2: Fold the loose edges about 1/2 inch back along the dotted lines, as illustrated to the right.

Result: The Nile River

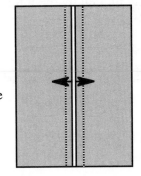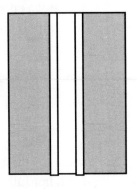

Fold #3: Fold the four corners to the middle, tucking the outside edges under the narrow bands created in Fold #2.

Result: Making a basket.

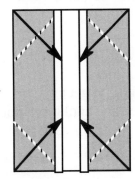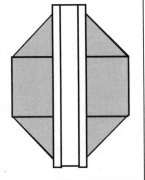

Fold #4: Fold the upper end down, and the lower end up along the dotted lines. Overlap as shown.

Fold here.

Fold here.

Result: Wrapping a baby.

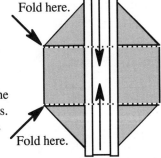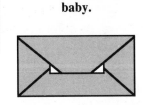

Fold #5: Unfold the last step and insert your thumbs, gently pulling the right and left sides apart. The figure will open into a box. Press the edges to further define its shape.

Result: Baby Moses' basket

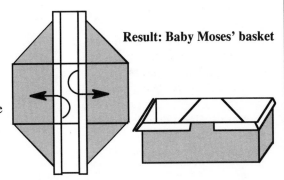

that it was partly hidden by the long grasses. She told the baby's big sister, Miriam, to hide along the river bank and watch what would happen to the basket.

Soon Pharaoh's daughter came down to the Nile River to take a bath. She saw the basket in the long grasses and asked her helpers to get it.

When Pharaoh's daughter looked inside, the baby was crying. She felt sorry for the baby and understood that it must be a Hebrew boy being hidden from her father.

Just then, Miriam came out of hiding and said, "Shall I go and find you a Hebrew nurse?"

Pharaoh's daughter said, "Yes. Go."

Miriam ran to get their mother who was hired by Pharaoh's daughter to take care of the baby until he was old enough to come and live in the palace. Pharaoh's daughter named the baby Moses, which means, "saved from the waters."

Raised by his real Hebrew mother and educated by the finest Egyptian teachers, Moses was well prepared to eventually grow up to become one God's greatest leaders.

Summary of folding directions

Preliminary fold: Fold a rectangle in half along the dotted line as shown below. Then unfold for Fold #1.

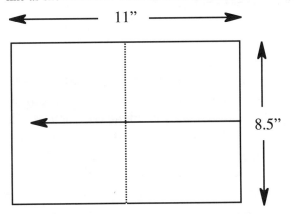

Fold #1: Fold the right and left sides to the middle crease that was created in the preliminary fold. Press firmly along the dotted lines.

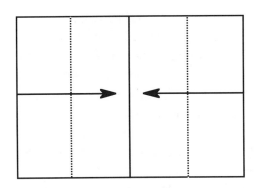

Fold #2: Fold the loose edges about 1/2 inch back along the dotted lines.

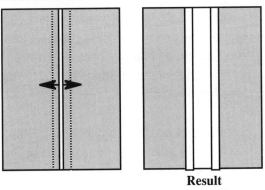

Result

Fold #3: Fold the 4 corners to the middle, tucking the outside edges under the narrow bands created in Fold #2.

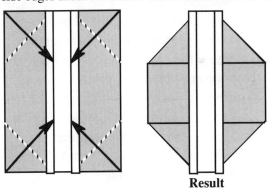

Result

Fold #4: Fold the upper end down, and the lower end up along the dotted lines. Overlap as shown.

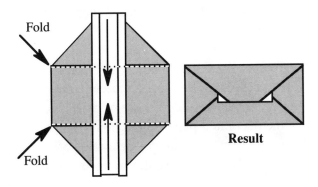

Result

Fold #5: Unfold the last step and insert your thumbs, gently pulling the right and left sides apart. The figure will open into a box. Press the edges to further define its shape.

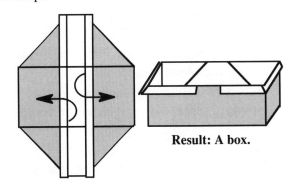

Result: A box.

Optional follow-up activities for "Baby In A Basket"

1. After telling the story, review the sequence of folds used to construct a paper basket, or box. Emphasize the correct order, giving each step its name from the story: field, great double doors, Nile River, etc. When the story events and folds are paired or associated, memory for both is tremendously enhanced.

    With a fresh, unfolded piece of paper, reconstruct the box for your group, asking them to identify each step and tell you what comes next. If group members can't remember the next step, don't simply give them the answer. Instead, offer them a hint by referring back to the story in order to reinforce the paired associations: "What did Moses' mother make to protect him from the Nile River? Yes, a basket. Let's fold the four corners in like this…"

    As you reconstruct the box, emphasize the need to slowly line up the edges, pressing the creases firmly and completely. Distribute paper *only* after your group is confident about the folding procedure. Then fold the first box together as a group, step by step, continuing to identify each step by its name from the story. Don't be surprised when individual group members produce boxes of different dimensions. The resulting box size is determined by the width of the narrow bands (the Nile River) in Fold #3. *Accept and admire all efforts*. Uniformity between individuals is not essential.

2. The basic origami box featured in this story can be constructed from rectangles of any size or dimension, including squares. The copy paper size was used because it is readily available, without having to cut paper ahead of time. After the folding sequence is learned, experiment with papers of different sizes and textures, making sure to follow the same folding procedure each time.

3. Create long shallow boxes by making the preliminary fold divide the paper in half along its horizontal midline, rather than the vertical midline, as in this story. All other steps remain the same.

4. Box lids can be made by increasing the width of the narrow bands created in Fold #3. The basic directions suggest that the bands be 1/2 inch wide. If you slightly increase the width of the band to 3/4 inch, the resulting box will be slightly larger. It will slip over the top of the basic box, providing a snugly fitting cover. Looser fitting lids can be made by doubling the width of the bands, from 1/2 inch to one inch.

5. Decorate a finished box with basket weaving designs. Then make the same designs on another unfolded piece of paper. Fold the decorated paper into a box. Compare it to the first box that was decorated after it was folded. How are the two boxes differ-

ent? How are they alike? Decide if it is more efficient to decorate paper before it is folded, or when the box is complete. Does it make a difference which side of the paper is facing up when you begin? Experiment with different starting positions.

6. Make boxes as gifts, to contain gifts, or as useful storage bins for your storytelling location. Decorate with flowers, stickers, or symbolic cut-outs. Try making a box to hold your bible.

7. Moses' mother wrapped her most precious gift and placed it into the basket that she made. Ask your group members to decide what their most precious gift is (talent, skill, or possession), draw a picture of it, fold it up, and place it inside the paper baskets that they have constructed. Allow group members to choose whether or not they want to sign their names. Share the groups' answers by placing all of the baskets on a table and mixing them up. Then ask volunteers to come up, close their eyes, pick one, and show it to the group. Some groups may want to speculate about who drew the pictures, but others will want to remain anonymous. Discuss what great gifts Moses gave us, such as the concept of one God, the ten commandments, and a day of rest.

8. Will paper boxes float? Are they waterproof? Moses' mother sealed her basket with mud and pitch. This was necessary because the woven bulrushes were loosely connected. The microscopic fibers in paper, however, are very tight in comparison. But some papers are not as tightly constructed as others. To demonstrate the differences, make boxes from a soft construction paper (loose fibers), regular copy paper (medium fibers), and a crisp linen stationery (tight fibers). Float each box in water. Compare the relative sogginess at regular intervals (every five minutes) until one of them falls apart.

Fiber tightness is not the only difference to consider in waterproofing. What the fibers are made of is possibly more important. To demonstrate this concept, make boxes from aluminum foil, cotton fabric (use a hot iron to make the creases), and regular copy paper. Float them as before.

After these experiments, test acquired knowledge by sponsoring a contest to see who can create the most waterproof box. Divide into teams. Give each team identical materials to select from (various types of papers, glue, paste, dirt, etc.) and 15 minutes to apply their knowledge of fiber content and tightness in constructing the most waterproof box. Find the winner through a float test. Award the winning team with a privilege, such as being first to get snacks, extra play time, or not having to clean up.

9. Retell the story, but dramatize the various roles. Ask for volunteers to act out Pharaoh, Pharaoh's daughter, her helpers, Miriam, Moses' mother, the soldiers, and the remaining group members can be the Hebrew slaves. Improvise costumes or use puppets, as shown on page 37. As the narrator tells the story, the group pantomimes or acts out the actions. Allow the characters to add appropriate lines of dialog. Present to another group or video tape for viewing during snack time, or to show parents and/or visitors an example of the types of activities the group enjoys.

10. Examine the religious and historical significance of this story. Summarize the future events that occurred because Moses survived. Organize these consequences by making a time line beginning with the rescue of Moses from the water. Use the events on the time line to structure upcoming lessons.

11. Study the story from the differing points of view of each of the main characters: Pharaoh, Miriam, Moses' mother, and Pharaoh's daughter. Why did they act the way that they did? What motivated them? How did they feel? What fears did they have? Was there anything that they all had in common? Did the female characters share feelings that Pharaoh did not?

12. Use the story to introduce or complement discussions or lessons about:

a. The life of Moses.
b. Egyptian history.
c. The political and cultural importance of the Nile River.
d. The binding love between mother and child.
e. The hardships suffered by the Hebrew slaves.

Date	Group	Notes

Pull the paper and watch the wheat grow! The newspaper crown, a symbol of Ruth's great-grandson King David, is made from the top section of the spike of wheat.

R U T H   A N D   N A O M I

About the story:

Naomi and her daughter-in-law, Ruth, return to Bethlehem and survive by gathering grain from the fields of a wealthy relative. *Based on Ruth 1 - 4.*

Recommended ages:

Listening and paperfolding: age 4 through adult.

Required materials:

A stack of full-sized newspapers.
Scissors.
Stapler.

Optional introductory statement:

"I'm going to tell you the story of how two women helped each other overcome hardship and sorrow. Watch carefully as I use newspaper as part of the story. The name of the story is…"

Ruth and Naomi

A Story of Loyalty, Courage, and Love Ruth 1 - 4

Before there were kings in Israel and the judges ruled the land, there was a terrible famine where the people did not have enough food to eat. A young man and his wife, Naomi, and their two sons left their home near Bethlehem to go to another land called Moab, where there was plenty of food to eat.

Not long after the family settled into their new home in Moab, the man died, leaving his wife, Naomi, to take care of their two sons by herself. Eventually the sons married two women from Moab by the name of Orpah and Ruth.

Naomi, her sons, and their wives lived happily in Moab for about ten years. But then tragedy struck Naomi again. Both of her sons died, leaving Naomi alone with Orpah and Ruth. Naomi had no grandchildren, for neither Ruth nor Orpah had children.

By this time, the famine in Israel was ended and the people were no longer starving. So Naomi decided to return to her homeland near Bethlehem. When the three of them had traveled as far as the land of Judah, Naomi knew that it was time for them to go their separate ways.

"Go back to your mothers' houses," she said to her daughters-in-law, Orpah and Ruth. "May the Lord deal kindly with you, as you have dealt with me." She sadly kissed them good-bye.

They all hugged each other and Orpah and Ruth begin to cry. "No, we will return with you

---

Before you begin:
Cut a full newspaper section in half length-wise, so that each half measures about 11" wide and 27" long. Set it aside for storytelling.

---

to your people," they said.

But Naomi insisted that they go back. Naomi was old and had no more sons to offer them as husbands. She thought that they would have better lives if they returned home to their own families and customs.

Orpah sadly agreed and returned to Moab. But Ruth held on to Naomi and said, "Wherever you go, I will go, and wherever you live, I will live. Your people will be my people, and your God will be my God. Only death will part us."

Naomi saw that Ruth was determined to stay with her, so the two of them continued on to Bethlehem. They arrived just as the barley harvest was beginning. Ruth volunteered to go into the fields and gather some leftover grains so that they would have food to eat. She worked tirelessly, <u>gathering and gathering</u>.

Begin rolling the newspaper on the words, "gathering and gathering." Continue rolling as you tell the story until both sections of newspaper are rolled, then make the cuts as shown on the next page.

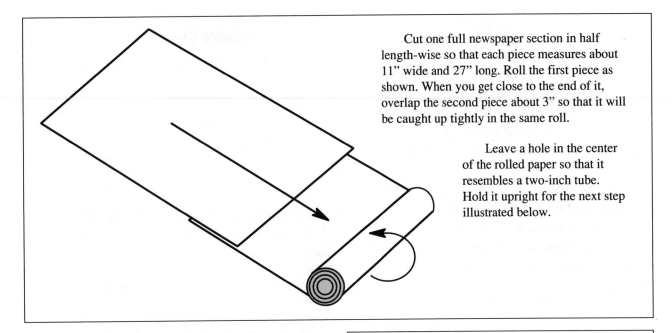

Cut one full newspaper section in half length-wise so that each piece measures about 11" wide and 27" long. Roll the first piece as shown. When you get close to the end of it, overlap the second piece about 3" so that it will be caught up tightly in the same roll.

Leave a hole in the center of the rolled paper so that it resembles a two-inch tube. Hold it upright for the next step illustrated below.

Boaz, a wealthy farmer and the owner of the field where Ruth worked, came out to watch the harvest. He was a relative of Naomi's husband. Boaz asked who the young woman was, gathering in his fields. He spoke kindly to Ruth and offered to let her continue to gather grain, for he had heard how she had bravely left her own family in order to take care of Naomi. He secretly instructed his workers to leave extra stalks of grain just for Ruth to pick up.

So Ruth continued to gather and gather during all the rest of the days of the barley harvest and then began to gather <u>wheat</u> as well.

On the word, "wheat" pull up on the middle part of the newspaper to form a spike of wheat.

It wasn't long before the wealthy Boaz asked Ruth to be his wife. After they were married, Ruth and Boaz had a son, so that at last, Naomi became a happy grandmother.

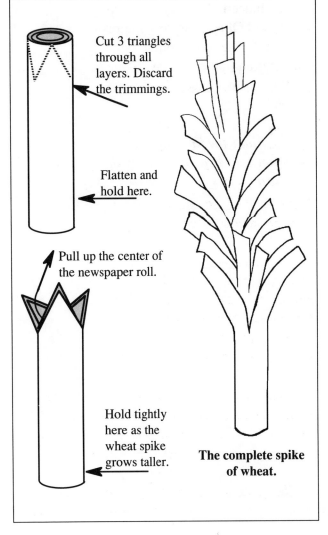

Cut 3 triangles through all layers. Discard the trimmings.

Flatten and hold here.

Pull up the center of the newspaper roll.

Hold tightly here as the wheat spike grows taller.

The complete spike of wheat.

Pull out the top strip of newspaper from the spike of wheat and begin folding the crown. Staple the crown together just as you finish saying the last words of the story.

The women of Bethlehem told Naomi, "The baby shall restore your life and nourish your old age, for your daughter-in-law, Ruth, who loves you and is better to you than seven sons, has given birth to him."

Indeed, the baby, who was named Obed, was very important, for he turned out to become the grandfather of David, one of the greatest <u>kings</u> Israel ever had!

Place the finished crown upon your head as you say the word "kings."

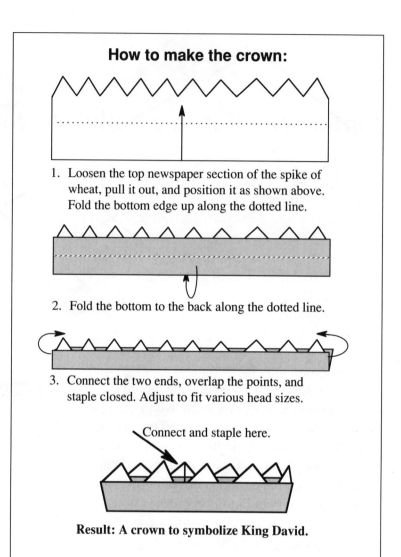

How to make the crown:

1. Loosen the top newspaper section of the spike of wheat, pull it out, and position it as shown above. Fold the bottom edge up along the dotted line.

2. Fold the bottom to the back along the dotted line.

3. Connect the two ends, overlap the points, and staple closed. Adjust to fit various head sizes.

Connect and staple here.

Result: A crown to symbolize King David.

Optional follow-up activities for "Ruth and Naomi"

1. Bring enough old newspapers so that everyone in your group can make his or her own spike of wheat and crown. Avoid passing out scissors or paper until after you have told the story. If your time is limited, or you do not have enough scissors to go around, simply pre-cut the newspaper sections. Because newspaper is so thin, several sections can efficiently be cut at one time. Scissors can easily be shared for the triangle cuts because your group members will roll their newspapers at different rates. Hold the crowns together and try them on before stapling for proper sizing.

2. Try creating a giant spike of wheat by letting each group member contribute a piece of newspaper. This activity emphasizes the spirit of cooperation and demonstrates that when a group works together toward a common goal, the results can be amazing and very satisfying. Procedure:

   a. Arrange the group in a circle on the floor, in chairs, or at tables that are angled so that everyone can make eye-contact with each other. Seeing each other builds group unity.

   b. Distribute one full newspaper section to every other group member. If you have an odd number of members, work with the last person yourself.

   c. Ask the members with the paper to work together with the person sitting next to them to cut the full section in half. Each of them will end up with one half of the newspaper. Do not be concerned if different partners cut the newspapers crookedly or in slightly different widths. These variations do not effect the final outcome.

   d. Choose one person to begin rolling his or her newspaper. Make your selection according to correctly answered questions from the lesson, such as, *"Who can name the part of the Bible that this story comes from?"* or *"Who can tell us the names of Naomi's daughters-in-law?"*

   e. When the first person has rolled his or her newspaper to within three or four inches of the end, pass it to the next person in the circle so that the next section of newspaper can be overlapped and rolled. Continue passing the roll around until every person has added a piece. Whisper, "Gathering and gathering. Gathering and gathering…" as the paper roll becomes thicker and bulkier.

   f. After all pieces have been overlapped and rolled, select another group member to make the triangular cuts. Use a large, sharp scissors. (If all you have are the short school scissors, cut only a few layers at a time.) Discard the triangular scraps.

   g. Select another group member to begin pulling out the wheat with a gentle tug. Then pass it along so that everyone has a turn at tugging. If the tugs have been gentle enough, it is possible to circulate the giant wheat twice around the group.

   h. Measure the resulting wheat "tree." Say, "We made this *together*. What great teamwork!"

3. Experiment with other papers, such as freezer wrap, gift wrap, packing paper, picnic table covers, or the large rolls that are found in paper supply stores. Stiff construction paper does not pull up well for the spike of wheat, and soft construction paper tears easily. But both types of construction paper are adequate for the crown.

4. Use a large map during storytelling to point to Bethlehem, Judah, and the region of Moab.

5. When several pieces of newspaper are rolled simultaneously, the resulting crinkling sounds are merry and remarkable. Challenge your group to keep their voices silent during the group newspaper rolling as you tape record the sound. Play it back. Use it as background "music" for future tellings.

6. Retell the story, but this time, dramatize it by letting group members assume the roles of Naomi, her husband and sons, Ruth and Orpah, Boaz, and the Bethlehem women. Encourage the characters to add appropriate lines of dialog. Use the groups' spikes of wheat as props. Videotape for viewing during snacks or later, for parents or visitors.

7. Keep the crowns on hand for recognizing special accomplishments or for practicing leadership and decision-making skills. Select a group member to be king or queen of the day. Ask them to be in charge of leading activities or delegating responsibilities.

8. Use the crowns and spikes of wheat for Passover or Psalm Sunday celebrations. Organize a parade.

9. Use the story to introduce or complement discussions or lessons about:
   a. Famine: causes, solutions, current examples of.
   b. Hebrew marriage traditions and laws.
   c. Loyalty to family and traditions.
   d. The courage required to make changes.
   e. Family bonds and responsibilities.
   f. The difficulties associated with widowhood.
   g. King David.

Date	Group	Notes

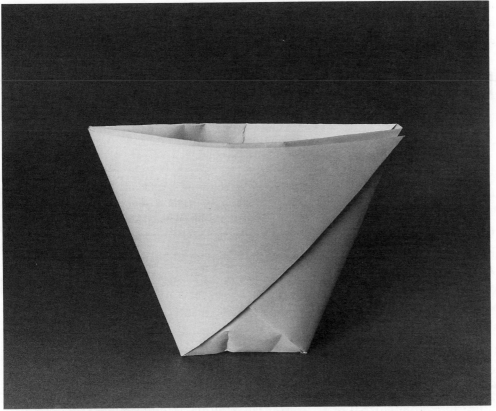

This traditional cup represents the widow's jar of oil that lasted throughout the drought. Folding directions are summarized on page 56.

E L I J A H   A N D   T H E   F A M I N E

About the story:

The Prophet Elijah is miraculously fed by ravens and then by a poor widow woman during a drought brought about by the king and queen's wickedness. *Based on 1 Kings 16:29 - 17:16.*

Recommended ages:

Listening and paperfolding: age 4 through adult.

Required materials:

One square of paper at least eight inches on each side, folded into a cup and then completely unfolded for storytelling.

Optional introductory statement:

"I'm going to tell you the story of how God helped the Prophet Elijah survive during a terrible drought. Watch carefully as I fold paper into different shapes. This is called origami, or Japanese paperfolding. The name of the story is…"

Elijah and the Famine   *1 Kings 16:29 - 17:16*

In the years 874 to 852 B. C., an evil king by the name of Ahab ruled Israel. King Ahab married Jezebel, the daughter of a foreign king. Jezebel did not believe in the Lord, the God of Israel. Instead, she worshiped a false God named Baal and with King Ahab's help, built an altar in Baal's honor. The Prophet Elijah was sent by God to speak out against Baal and to convince King Ahab to go back to worshiping the Lord, the God of Israel.

But King Ahab would not change. He continued to be one of the most wicked kings that Israel had ever had. So Elijah announced the Lord's punishment by saying, "As the Lord God of Israel lives, before whom I stand, there shall not be dew or rain these years, except by my word."

Without rain, the crops would not grow. Soon there was a famine where there was not enough food and the people began to starve. King Ahab and Queen Jezebel blamed Elijah for the drought and searched for him...

Everywhere. *(Point to all places on the square of paper, representing a search everywhere.)*

They looked high and low. *(Fold #1, pointing to the top and bottom of the triangle.)*

They looked to the east. *(Fold #2, pointing east.)*

Fold #1: With the wrong side facing up (the side that you want on the *inside* of your cup), fold a square in half along the diagonal dotted line.

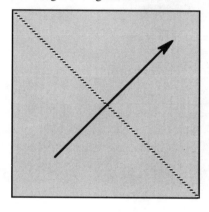

Result: A triangle. Point to the top and bottom, representing high and low.

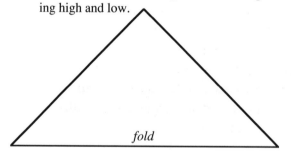

fold

Fold #2: Fold the left point over to the right edge and crease along the dotted line as shown.

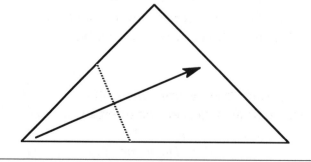

They looked to the west. *(Fold #3, pointing west.)* But the evil King Ahab and Queen Jezebel could not find Elijah anywhere.

The Lord protected Elijah by telling him to hide by a brook where he could drink the water and be fed by the ravens.

Unfold #2 and #3 to a triangle with creases in it. Hold the triangle as shown in the illustration to the lower right and wave it gently up and down so that the triangle tips represent a raven in flight.

The ravens brought him bread and meat in the morning and evening. To cool his throat, Elijah drank the sweet water of the brook. But after a while, the little river dried up because there was still no rain in Israel, for King Ahab and Queen Jezebel had not changed their wicked ways.

So the Lord sent Elijah to the city of Zarephath, north of Israel along the coast of the Mediterranean Sea. He was told that a widow, a woman who was living on her own because her husband had died, would feed and protect him while he was there.

As soon as Elijah arrived in Zarephath, he saw a woman out gathering sticks for a fire.

Fold the raven wings back to Fold #3, as though the wings were arms, gathering the sticks.

He said, "Please, bring me a little water to drink, and also a bit of bread."

Fold #3: Fold the right point over to the left edge and crease along the dotted line as shown.

Result:

Fold #2 and #3 opened up

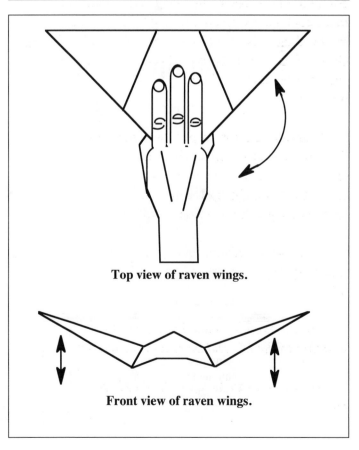

Top view of raven wings.

Front view of raven wings.

55

But she was very poor and had nothing baked. "I have only a handful of flour and this small jar of oil. *(Hold up Fold #4.)* I am gathering a couple of sticks, so that I may go in to build a fire to bake for myself and my son. We shall eat and then we shall die, for we have no more food."

"Don't be afraid," said Elijah. "Use the flour and oil to bake me a little cake, and then make more for yourself and your son. For the Lord the God of Israel says that the flour will not run out and the jar of oil shall not empty until the day that the Lord makes it rain upon the earth."

She did as Elijah said, and they all ate for many days. The flour did not run out and the jar of oil lasted, according to the word of the Lord.

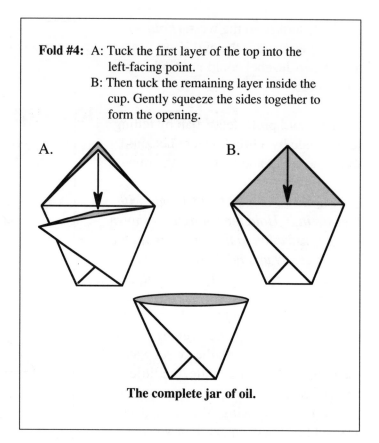

Fold #4: A: Tuck the first layer of the top into the left-facing point.
B: Then tuck the remaining layer inside the cup. Gently squeeze the sides together to form the opening.

The complete jar of oil.

Summary of folding directions

Fold #1: With the wrong side facing up, fold a square in half along the diagonal dotted line.

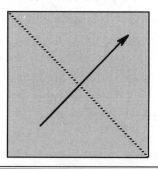

Fold #2: Fold the left point over to the right edge and crease along the dotted line.

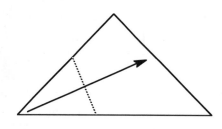

Fold #3: Fold the right point over to the left edge and crease along the dotted line.

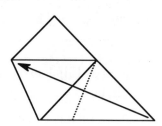

Fold #4: Tuck the first layer of the top into the left-facing point. Then tuck the remaining layer inside the cup. Gently squeeze the sides together to form the opening.

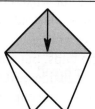

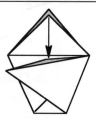

Result: The complete cup

Optional follow-up activities for "Elijah and the Famine"

1. After the story is told, pull the cup apart and reconstruct it for the group, being careful to identify the steps according to their names in the story: searching high and low, east and west, gathering sticks, and finally the complete jar of oil. Distribute practice paper and fold the first cup together as a group. The triangle formed in Fold #1 should be folded as precisely as possible so that the cup will fit together at the end. This figure is one of the simplest designs in origami and is often the first model that beginners learn to fold. Pass out smaller and smaller squares to make ever smaller cups. This increases precision and stimulates practice.

2. Fold a cup from newspaper or large construction paper that is 18 - 22 inches on each side. Decorate it, turn it upside down, and you have a fancy hat. Personalize with feathers, stickers, paper symbols, lettering, or other materials. Have a style show or parade where each artist can be recognized and applauded for their creative efforts. Display them together on a hat tree or use as fancy baskets.

3. Being careful to use clean scissors and a sterile folding surface, pre-cut waxed paper or freezer wrap into squares and fold into triangles. Make enough for your entire group. Let them finish the cups, but warn against dirty fingers on the insides. At snack time, or as a special treat, fill the cups with something to drink.

4. Use a large map during storytelling to point to Tishbe in Gilead (where Elijah was born), the brook Cherith (east of the Jordan where the ravens fed him), and Zarephath (where the widow fed him).

5. Make adult-sized finger puppets from cups folded out of two-inch squares, and child-sized puppets from cups folded out of one-inch squares. Invert and place them on your fingertips like thimbles. Add facial features to the cup itself, and/or draw faces with water-based markers directly on your finger, using the cup as the puppet's hat. Create several different characters.

6. Retell the story, but this time, dramatize it by letting group members assume the roles of Elijah, King Ahab, Queen Jezebel, the ravens, and the widow. Encourage the characters to add appropriate lines of dialog. Use the groups' cups as jars of oil or hats for the characters. Videotape for viewing later during snacks or as a demonstration for parents or visitors.

7. Retell the story using finger puppets created in suggestion #5.

8. Compare this story to the miracle of Hanukkah. Both stories relate how a jar of oil lasted and both involve a conflict between Hebrew and pagan religions. Explore their historical ramifications.

9. Make several cups to fill with gifts or treats to share with another group, give to shut-ins, present to parents, or simply to take home.

10. When several tiny cups (made from two-inch paper or smaller) are strung together with yarn or string, a colorful chain or necklace results. Make one group necklace where each group member contributes a piece, or let each individual create their own. Make matching earrings by attaching to old posts or clip-ons.

11. Use the story to introduce or complement discussions or lessons about:
    a. Famine: causes, solutions, and current examples of.
    b. Elijah's many other accomplishments.
    c. King Ahab's conflicting loyalties.
    d. The miracles in this story and those associated with the widow's son. Relate to miracles experienced by your group.
    e. References to Jezebel throughout literature and the type of character she represents.

Date	Group	Notes

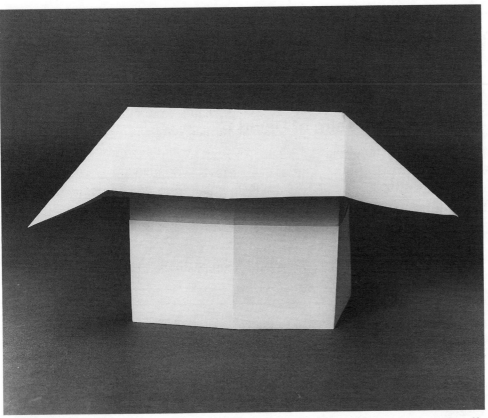

This simple house is folded in only four steps. Folding directions are summarized on page 63.

T H E   L O R D   I S   M Y   S H E P H E R D

About the story:

The Twenty-third Psalm is uniquely illustrated with progressive paperfolding until at last, the "house of the Lord" emerges. *Based entirely on Psalms 23.*

Recommended ages:

Listening only: age 4 through adult.
Listening and paperfolding: age 6 through adult.

Required materials:

One square of paper at least six inches on each side, completely folded into the house and then unfolded for storytelling.

Optional introductory statement:

Watch carefully as I fold paper during the familiar prayer, the 23rd Psalm. This style of paperfolding is called origami, an ancient art form developed in Japan.

Psalms 23
A Psalm of David

The Lord is my shepherd,
I shall not want;
He makes me lie down in
<u>green pastures</u>.

On the words, "green pastures," hold the square as in Step #1.

He leads me beside <u>still waters</u>;

On the words, "still waters," make a slight water wave in the square as in Step #2.

He restores my soul.
He leads me in paths of
righteousness for His
name's sake.

Even though I walk through
the <u>valley</u> of the shadow of
death,

On the word, "valley," hold up Step #3.

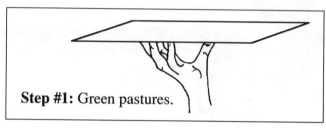

Step #1: Green pastures.

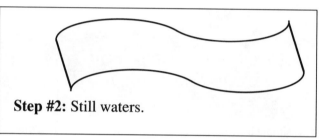

Step #2: Still waters.

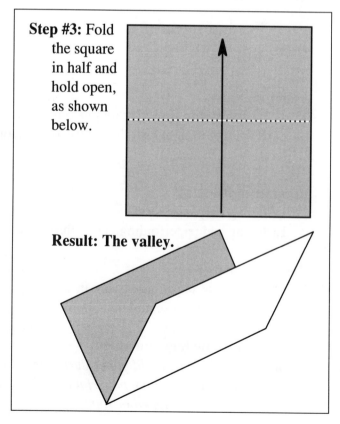

Step #3: Fold the square in half and hold open, as shown below.

Result: The valley.

I fear no evil;
for Thou art with me;
Thy rod and Thy staff,
they comfort me.

Thou prepares a <u>table</u> before
me in the presence of my
enemies;

*On the word, "table," hold
up Step #4.*

Thou anoints my head with
oil,
my <u>cup</u> overflows.

*On the word, "cup," panto-
mime overflowing or falling
water motions with Step #5.*

Step #4: Fold the top and the bottom edges to the center midline that was created in Step #3. Position like a table. Then close the table and flip it over to the other side for Step #5.

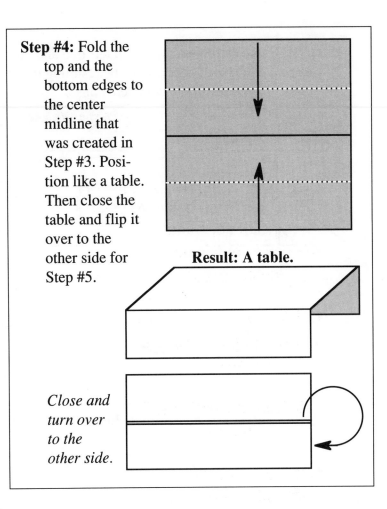

Result: A table.

Close and turn over to the other side.

Step #5: Fold the figure in half, unfold, and then bring the right and left sides to the middle, creasing through all layers along the dotted lines as shown.

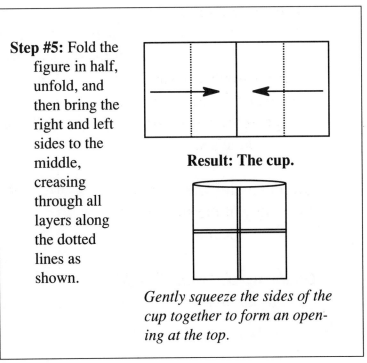

Result: The cup.

Gently squeeze the sides of the cup together to form an opening at the top.

Step #6: Slip a thumb under the top left flap and pull the corner out and over to the left. Repeat on the right side. Press the resulting triangles firmly. Then flip the figure over to the other side for the complete house.

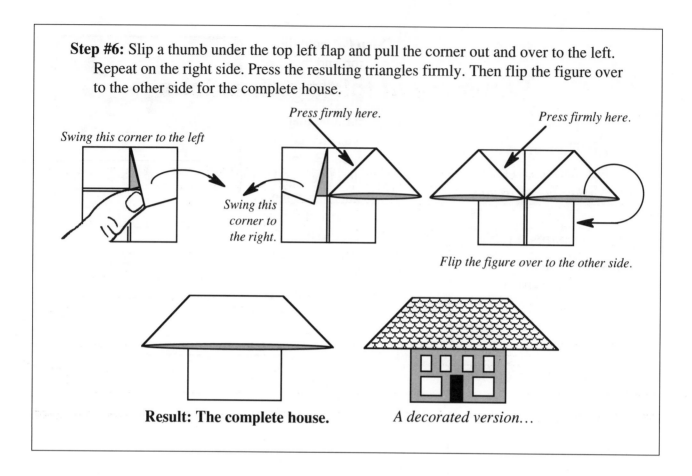

Surely goodness and mercy shall follow me
all the days of my life;
and I shall dwell in the <u>house</u> of the Lord forever.

On the word, "house," hold up Step #6.

Summary of folding directions

Fold #1: Fold a square in half and then unfold for the next step.

Fold #2: Fold the top and the bottom edges to the center midline that was created in Fold #1. Flip it over to the other side for the next step.

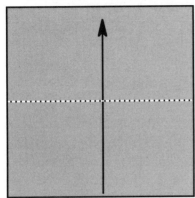

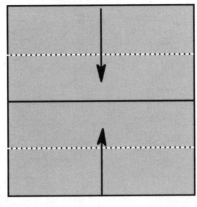

Result: Flip to the other side.

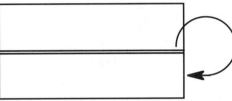

Fold #3: Fold the figure in half to create a middle guideline, unfold, and then bring the right and left sides to the middle, creasing through all layers along the dotted lines.

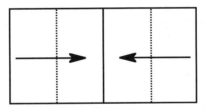

Result

Fold #4: Slip a thumb under the top left flap and pull the corner out and over to the left. Repeat on the right side. Press the resulting triangles firmly. Then flip the figure over to the other side for the complete house.

Swing this corner to the left

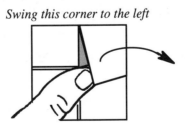

Press firmly here.

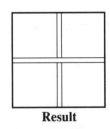

Swing this corner to the right.

Press firmly here.

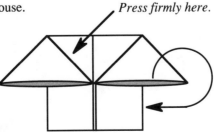

Flip the figure over to the other side.

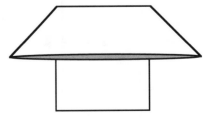

Result: The complete house.

Optional follow-up activities for "Psalms 23"

1. After reciting the verse, review the sequence of folds used to construct the house. Emphasize the correct order, giving each step its name from the poem: green pastures, valley, table, cup, and finally, the house. With a fresh, unfolded piece of paper, reconstruct the house for your group, asking them to identify each step and tell you what comes next. As you fold the house, emphasize how to line up the edges before creasing firmly. Distribute paper *only* after your group is confident about the folding procedure. Then fold the first house together as a group, step by step, reciting the verse together as you fold. *Note:* A common error is forgetting to flip the table over before folding the cup. Watch out for this mistake.

2. After the folding sequence is learned, try folding houses from smaller and smaller squares, following the same procedure each time. Precision and memory will increase with each attempt.

3. Decorate a finished house. Then make similar designs on another, unfolded piece of paper. Fold the decorated paper into a house. Compare it to the first house that was decorated after it was folded. Observe differences and similarities. Is it better to decorate paper before it is folded, or when the figure is complete?

4. Use the little houses as nametags, ornaments, place marks, or lace with yarn for necklaces. This house is also useful as a basic building prop for puppet shows.

5. Display your group's houses on a bulletin board like a map, or combine them to make a free-standing village. Add distinguishing features like towers or symbols. Set them on a cardboard base. Model the street patterns after your community, a historic city, or invent an entirely new neighborhood.

6. Perform the poem with all group members reciting and folding together simultaneously. Prefold the houses, and then completely unfold them for the group performance. Present for another group or videotape for later viewing.

7. Examine the pronouns in this verse. Point out that when everything is good, God is in the third person (He). When things are difficult, God becomes closer and we address God in the second person (Thou, or You).

Date	Group	Notes

Jiggle the tail fins and watch the jaws snap! Folding directions for this playful fish are summarized on page 69.

About the story:

Jonah tries to disobey God by sailing away to hide. When the sailors throw him into the stormy sea, he is swallowed by a big fish. *Based on Jonah 1 - 3.*

Recommended ages:

Listening only: age 4 through adult.
Listening and paperfolding: age 6 through adult.

Required materials:

One square of paper at least six inches on each side, folded into a big fish and then completely unfolded for storytelling, and a dark colored marker to draw eyes (optional).

Optional introductory statement:

"I'm going to tell you a story of how a man tries to disobey God and then run away. Watch carefully as I fold paper into different shapes. This is called origami, or Japanese paperfolding. The name of the story is…"

Jonah and the Big Fish *Jonah 1 - 3*

Before You Begin:
Fold a square in half along its diagonal center, forming a triangle. Unfold the triangle for storytelling. The diagonal crease provides a midline for Fold #1. In origami, this preparatory step is called a preliminary fold.

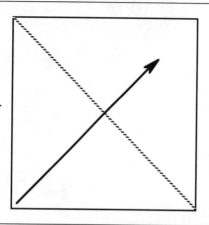

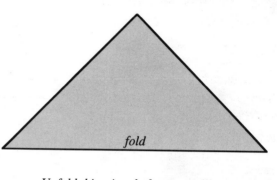

Unfold this triangle for storytelling.

Once, a long, long time ago, God told a man named Jonah to go and warn the wicked people living in Ninevah, an evil city, that they should stop being so bad or God was going to destroy their city. But Jonah did not want to go to that bad place. He was afraid that the people might not like him for bringing such terrible news. Besides, it was far away, and he knew that God was merciful and was probably going to forgive them. Jonah believed that God would not really destroy the whole city, and then the people in Ninevah would think he was a liar.

So, instead of obeying God, Jonah tried to hide and run away. He went to the sea and bought a ticket to ride in a ship that had a sail that looked something like this *(demonstrate with Fold #1)*. Jonah hoped that the ship would take him far away from Ninevah and that God would not be able to find him.

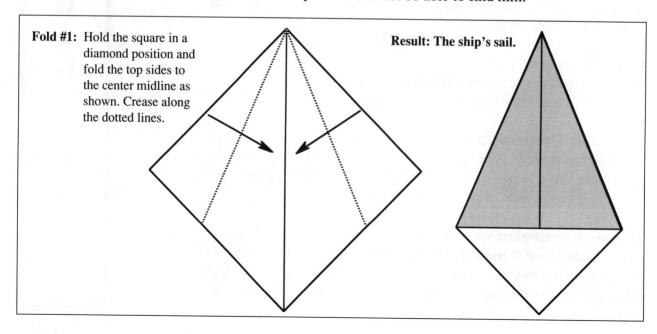

Fold #1: Hold the square in a diamond position and fold the top sides to the center midline as shown. Crease along the dotted lines.

Result: The ship's sail.

While Jonah was asleep in the inner part of the ship, a terrible storm came. Waves crashed over the ship and the sailors were afraid that the storm would break the sail, like this *(demonstrate with the broken sail of Fold #2)*.

The sailors were from different places and each prayed in his own way, but the storm did not stop. Then they threw cargo into the sea to make the ship lighter, but it still did not get better. Finally, the ship's captain found Jonah and woke him up so that he could pray, too.

The sailors questioned him, "Tell us, what do you do for a living? Where do you come from? What kind of people live there? How do they pray?"

Jonah said that he was a Hebrew and that he believed in the Lord, the God of Heaven, *(on the word "Heaven," demonstrate an upward motion with Fold #3)* who made the sea and the dry land. He told them that he had been trying to run away from God.

The sailors said, "What should we do to you to make the sea quiet down for us?"

Jonah said, "Take me and throw me into the water, then the sea will calm down. I know that it is because of me that this terrible storm has come upon you."

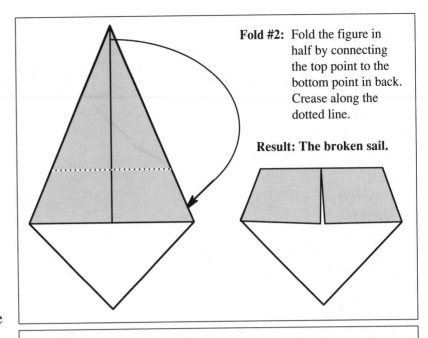

Fold #2: Fold the figure in half by connecting the top point to the bottom point in back. Crease along the dotted line.

Result: The broken sail.

Fold #3: Do two motions at the same time: push the right corner toward the center midline while pulling the loose flap straight up. A crease will form along the dotted line as indicated. Repeat for the left side.

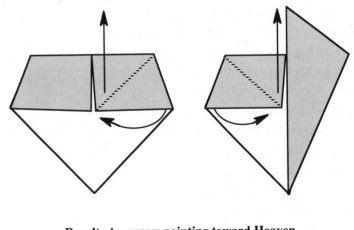

Result: An arrow pointing toward Heaven.

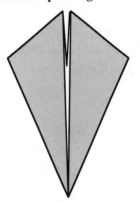

The sailors tried rowing harder to bring the ship back to land, but the waves got higher and higher. The sailors did not want to do it, but they decided that the only way to save the ship was to do as Jonah said. They took Jonah and threw him into the sea. The water calmed down immediately.

Then God made a great fish, that looked something like this *(demonstrate with Fold #4)* come along and swallow Jonah.

(Jiggle the tail fins of the fish so that the jaws open and close.)

He stayed in the belly of the fish for three days and three nights.

While Jonah was inside the fish, he prayed. God heard his prayers, and made the fish spit him out unto dry land. God then said, "Arise, go and proclaim the message that I tell you."

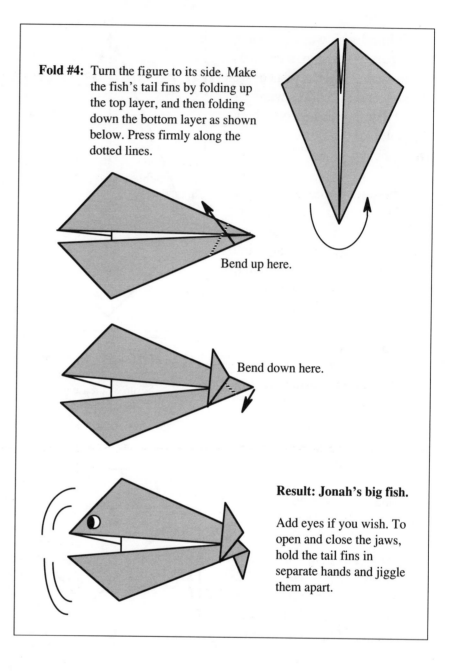

Fold #4: Turn the figure to its side. Make the fish's tail fins by folding up the top layer, and then folding down the bottom layer as shown below. Press firmly along the dotted lines.

Bend up here.

Bend down here.

Result: Jonah's big fish.

Add eyes if you wish. To open and close the jaws, hold the tail fins in separate hands and jiggle them apart.

Jonah learned his lesson. This time, Jonah obeyed and he went to the wicked city of Ninevah. There, the people listened to Jonah's warning and realized that they had been wrong. They were sorry and prayed for God's forgiveness. So God did not destroy the city, just as Jonah had predicted.

Summary of folding directions

Preliminary Fold: Fold a square in half along its diagonal center, forming a triangle. Then unfold the triangle for Fold #1.

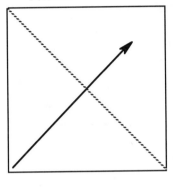

Fold #1: Position the square like a diamond and fold the top sides to the center midline. Crease along the dotted lines.

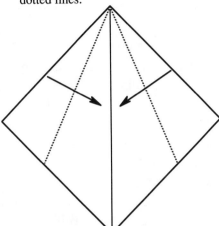

Fold #2: Fold the figure in half by connecting the top point to the bottom point in back. Crease along the dotted line.

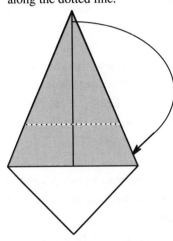

Fold #3: Do two motions at the same time: push the right corner toward the center midline while pulling the loose flap straight up. A crease will form along the dotted line as indicated. Repeat for the left side.

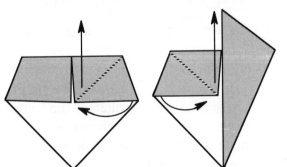

Fold #4: Turn the figure to its side. Make the fish's tail fins by folding up the top layer, and then folding down the bottom layer. Press firmly along the dotted lines.

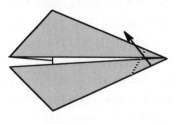

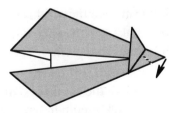

Result: A big fish.

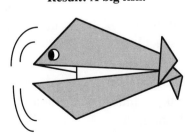

Optional follow-up activities for "Jonah and the Big Fish"

1. After the story is told, pull the fish apart and reconstruct it for your group, being careful to identify the steps according to their names in the story: the ship's sail, the broken sail, the arrow pointing to Heaven, and finally the big fish. Fold it again with fresh, unfolded paper to demonstrate how to crease thoroughly and precisely. This time, ask your group to be the teachers and tell you the folding steps. When they say the steps in unison, their auditory memory is reinforced.

   Distribute practice paper and fold the first fish together as a group. Then pass out smaller and smaller squares to make ever smaller fish. This reinforces memorization of the steps and the text, increases precision, and stimulates practice.

2. Decorate paper before folding. Guess where the markings will end up on the completed fish. Are they hidden inside the fish? Does it make a difference which side of the paper faces down when you begin folding? Next, decorate a finished fish. Unfold and analyze where the markings are on the flat paper. Put it back together and observe the decorative markings fall back into place.

3. Display the fish on a large bulletin board with a background depicting the sea. Other ways to use the fish are to make a group mobile, dangle them from the ceiling, arrange them in a simulated fish tank, or link them together like a colorful fish chain.

4. Use the fish as ornaments, nametags, jewelry, place markers, or bookmarks.

5. Use a large map during or after storytelling to point to Gath-hepher in Galilee (where Jonah was born), the port city of Joppa (where he bought passage), Tarshish (where he was running to), and Ninevah (where God told him to go in the first place).

6. Play Bible verse fish pond: Write different Bible verses on the *outside* of several fish, and the corresponding Bible book and verse on the *inside* of the fish. Attach a paper clip to each one. Make a fishing pole by tying a magnet to a string. Then attach the string to a ruler or a stick. Use a small swimming pool, fish tank, or large bowl as a pond for the fish.

   Let each group member take a turn at catching a fish from the pond. You may need to monitor the fishing since some magnets will pick up several at one time. Ask the fisherman to read the verse written on the fish and try to guess which part of the Bible it came from. Allow other group members to answer if necessary. Offer a reward to group members who take their fish home to memorize the verse and recite it correctly during the next session. Use verses you have recently studied. An alternative method is to simply write Bible names, events, or places (instead of verses) on the outsides of the fish, and their corresponding Bible stories on the fish's insides.

7. Fold puppets to represent the big fish and Jonah and the sailors (directions for people puppets are on page 37). Use a big box as a puppet theatre and create a scene at sea. Cover it with brown or green paper or fabric for the scenes on land. Make a ship (directions for an origami ship can be found on page 14 of *Holiday Folding Stories* - see page 73 for bibliographic data). Dramatize the story, allowing the characters to add appropriate lines of dialog. Perform for other groups or videotape for viewing at a later time. Save the puppet theatre for other performances.

8. Compare this story to other examples of Biblical disobedience. Include details relating to the consequences of disobeying. Ask group members to give examples from their own lives. Is disobeying ever the right thing to do?

9. Use the story to introduce or complement discussions or lessons about:

    a. Cities with wicked reputations: causes, tolerance of, solutions, current examples of.
    b. The rest of Jonah's story after God forgives the people of Nineveh.
    c. Obedience.
    d. Authority - who should be obeyed?
    e. Punishment, discipline, and consequences. What is natural? What is appropriate? What is inappropriate?
    f. Forgiveness from a merciful God.
    g. Fears related to what others may think.
    h. The benefits of prayer.

Date	Group	Notes

For more information....

National Organizations

The following groups provide members with informative newsletters, sponsor annual conventions, special events and festivals, and compile complete lists of regional groups, materials, and resources. Membership is inexpensive and easily obtained by inquiring at the addresses listed below.

National Association for the Preservation and Perpetuation of Storytelling (NAPPS), P. O. Box 309, Jonesborough, TN 37659. Phone 615-753-2171.

The Friends of The Origami Center of America, 15 West 77 St., New York, NY 10024-5192. Phone 212-769-5635.

Sources for material containing both paperfolding and text:

Flinn, Lisa and Younger, Barbara, 1992, *Making Scripture Stick: 52 Unforgettable Bible Verse Adventures*, p. 76-87, Loveland, CO: Group Books.

Kallevig, Christine Petrell, 1993, *All About Pockets: Storytime Activities For Early Childhood*, p. 40, Broadview Hts., OH: Storytime Ink International.

Kallevig, Christine Petrell, 1991, *Folding Stories: Storytelling and Origami Together As One*, Broadview Hts., OH: Storytime Ink Intl.

Kallevig, Christine Petrell, 1992, *Holiday Folding Stories: Storytelling and Origami Together For Holiday Fun*, Broadview Hts., OH: Storytime Ink International.

Murry and Rigney, 1928, *Paper Folding For Beginners*, Dover.

Pellowski, Anne, 1987, *Family Storytelling Handbook*, p. 74-84 (two stories written by Gay Merrill Gross), New York, NY: Macmillan Publishing Co.

Rey, H. A., 1952, *Curious George Rides A Bike*, New York, NY: Houghton.

Schimmel, Nancy, 1982, *Just Enough To Make A Story: A Sourcebook For Storytellers*, p. 20-32, Berkeley, CA: Sisters' Choice Press.

Books for beginning paperfolders:

Ayture-Scheele, Zulal, 1987, *The Great Origami Book*, New York, NY: Sterling Publishing Co.

Ayture-Scheele, Zulal, 1986, *Origami In Color: paperfolding fun*, New York, NY: Gallery Books.

Kobayashi, Kazuo and Yamaguchi, Makoto, 1987, *Origami for Parties*, New York: Kodansha International.

Lewis, Shari and Oppenheimer, Lillian, 1962, *Folding Paper Puppets,* New York, NY: Stein and Day Publishers

Lewis, Shari and Oppenheimer, Lillian, 1965, *Folding Paper Masks,* New York, NY: Dutton.

Randlett, Samuel, 1961, *The Best of Origami,* New York: E. P. Dutton & Co., Inc.

Sarasas, Claude, 1964, *The ABC's Of Origami,* Rutland, VT: Charles E. Tuttle, Inc.

Takahama, Toshie, 1985, *The Joy of Origami,* Tokyo, Japan: Shufunotomo/Japan Publications. (also by the same author: *Origami Toys, Origami for Fun, Quick and Easy Origami).*

Weiss, Stephen, 1984, *Wings & Things: origami that flies,* New York, NY: St. Martin's Press.

Books with historic information about origami:

Honda, Isao, 1965, *The World of Origami,* Rutland, VT: Japan Publications Trading Co.

Lang, Robert J., 1988, *The Complete Book of Origami,* New York, NY: Dover Publications, Inc.

Randlett, Samuel, 1961, *The Art of Origami,* New York, NY: E. P. Dutton & Co., Inc.

Books relating to storytelling techniques:

Greene, Ellin, *Storytelling: Art and Technique,* New York, NY: R. R. Bowker Co.

Herman, Gail, *Storytelling: A Triad in the Arts,* Mansfield Center, CT: Creative Learning Press.

Livo, Norma, *Storytelling: Process and Practice,* Englewood, CO: Libraries Unlimited.

Pellowski, Anne, 1987, *Family Storytelling Handbook,* New York, NY: Macmillan Publishing Co.

Schimmel, Nancy, 1982, *Just Enough To Make a Story: A Sourcebook For Storytelling,* Berkeley, CA: Sisters' Choice.

Christine Petrell Kallevig is available as a keynote speaker or to present Storigami demonstrations at conventions, workshops, assemblies, or festivals. Contact the publisher, Storytime Ink International, P. O. Box 470505, Broadview Heights, Ohio for details.

Index

Other titles available from

International

Holiday Folding Stories: Storytelling and Origami Together For Holiday Fun by Christine Petrell Kallevig: Nine original holiday stories illustrated by nine easy origami models for ages preschool through adult. Each story is based on historic holiday facts and traditions. The featured holidays are Columbus Day, Halloween, Thanksgiving, Hanukkah, Christmas, Valentine's Day, Easter, May Day, and Mother's Day. Includes holiday histories, extensive ideas for optional activities, complete illustrations and directions, photographs, glossary, and index. Recommended for storytellers, teachers, activity therapists, recreation leaders, and religious educators. ISBN 0-9628769-1-7 $11.50

Folding Stories: Storytelling and Origami Together As One by Christine Petrell Kallevig: Nine humorous short stories are combined with easy paperfolding techniques, for ages preschool through adult. Topics range from original folktales to modern day adventures, and are appropriate for any setting or season. *School Library Journal (June 1991)* said, "Each (story) is surrounded by apparatus designed to make the experience painless… Kallevig's evident enthusiasm for this captivating technique will inspire even the most hesitant beginner." Includes dozens of suggestions for optional activities, complete illustrations and directions, photographs, and index. Recommended for storytellers, teachers, paperfolders, activity therapists, and recreation leaders. ISBN 0-9628769-4-1 $11.50

All About Pockets: Storytime Activities For Early Childhood by Christine Petrell Kallevig: 128 pages of pocket poems, fingerplays, games, original two minute pocket stories (includes one folding story), songs, riddles, patterns, crafts, and pocket tricks. Every activity emphasizes the important eye-ear-hand-body-mind connectedness that defines the intellectual, social, and emotional abilities of young children. Easy to use, fun for kids age 3 through 6, and a perfect companion to storytelling aprons. Recommended for parents, preschool teachers, storytellers, children's librarians, and daycare providers. ISBN 0-9628769-6-8 $9.95

Use this coupon to order additional copies of *Bible Folding Stories: Old Testament Stories and Paperfolding Together As One*, or any of the other popular titles *(library patrons - please photocopy)*.

Name _____

Address _____

_____

City/State_____

Zip _____

title	Qty.	Price	Total
Folding Stories: Storytelling & Origami Together As One ISBN 0-9628769-0-9		$11.50	
Holiday Folding Stories: Storytelling & Origami Together For Holiday Fun ISBN 0-9628769-1-7		$11.50	
Bible Folding Stories: Old Testament Stories and Paperfolding Together As One ISBN 0-9628769-4-1		$11.50	
All About Pockets: Storytime Activities For Early Childhood ISBN 0-9628769-6-8		$9.95	
SUBTOTAL			
OH residents add 7% sales tax			
Postage & handling: Add $2 (1st book), $1 @ additional book			
US dollars only TOTAL ENCLOSED			

Mail to:
Storytime Ink International
P. O. Box 470505
Broadview Heights, OH 44147-0505

Allow 2-4 weeks for delivery